WE BELIEVED
WE WERE
IMMORTAL

Also By Kathleen Wickham

The Role of the Clarion-Ledger in the Adoption of the 1982 Education Reform Act: Winning the Pulitzer Prize (Lewiston, NY: Edwin Mellen Press, 2007).

Math Tools for Journalists (Oak Park, Ill: Marion Street Press, 2001, 2003).

Perspectives: Online Journalism (Boulder: CourseWise Publishing, 1998).

WE BELIEVED
WE WERE
IMMORTAL

*Twelve Reporters Who
Covered the 1962 Integration
Crisis at Ole Miss*

Karen —

KATHLEEN W. WICKHAM

Preface by Bob Schieffer

Kathleen Wickham

*Yoknapatawpha Press
Oxford, Mississippi*

Portions of this book previously appeared in the following publications:

"Steel Magnolia: Student Newspaper Editor Sidna Brower," *Journalism History*, 2017.

"Dean of the Civil Rights Reporters: A conversation with Claude Sitton," *Journalism History*, 2014.

"Murder in Mississippi: The Unresolved Case of Agence France-Presse's Paul Guihard," *Journalism History*, 2011.

The Role of the Clarion-Ledger in the Adoption of the 1982 Education Reform Act: Winning the Pulitzer Prize (Lewiston, NY: Edwin Mellen Press 2007).

ISBN 978-0-916242-83-1

Library of Congress Control Number: 2016957569

Printed in Korea

Book Layout & Design by Timothy K. Wickham (Fleuron Design Collective, LLC)

To the memory of Paul Guihard and the more than 300 journalists who covered the 1962 integration crisis at the University of Mississippi.

"We believed we were immortal and therefore nothing bad could happen to us."

Fred Powledge, Atlanta Journal-Constitution
April 1987

CONTENTS

TIMELINE

JANUARY 31, 1961: James Meredith submits letter of application to the University of Mississippi informing the registrar that he is not a white applicant.

FEBRUARY 4: University of Mississippi rejects James Meredith's application.

MAY 31: James Meredith files suit in federal court alleging his admission was denied based on race.

SEPTEMBER 10: Federal Court orders the university to admit Meredith. The case works its way through the courts to the U.S. Supreme Court.

SEPTEMBER 13, 1962: Gov. Ross Barnett declares "No school will be integrated in Mississippi."

SEPTEMBER 20: Barnett assumes the role of register and from offices on campus refuses to admit Meredith.

TUESDAY, SEPTEMBER 25: Barnett rejects Meredith from his office in Jackson after asking: "Which one of you is Meredith?" University officials, facing contempt charges, were prepared to admit Meredith.

WEDNESDAY, SEPTEMBER 26: Lieutenant Governor Paul Johnson, in Oxford, filling in for Barnett refuses to allow Meredith on campus.

THURSDAY, SEPTEMBER 27: Meredith's convoy turns back 40 miles from Oxford when reports of armed citizens and angry state patrolmen reach his escorts

FRIDAY, SEPTEMBER 28: Court of Appeals finds Barnett in civil contempt and orders Barnett personally fined $10,000 each day he prevents Meredith from registering. The deadline is October 2.

SEPTEMBER 29: The court found Lieutenant Governor Paul Johnson also in contempt. His personal fine was set at $5,000 a day. President Kennedy issued a legal proclamation citing his right to use federal officers to enforce the court's order. Barnett gives defiant speech at halftime of the Ole Miss-Kentucky football game in Jackson.

September 30:

2:25 P.M., First planeload of marshals arrives in Oxford.

4 P.M., Mississippi highway patrol controls campus entrances and marshals are stationed in front of the Lyceum.

5:30 P.M., Some 400 people are gathered near the Lyceum.

6 P.M., James Meredith is taken to his dormitory. Gravel and eggs are thrown at marshals.

7 P.M., Highway patrol abandons the entrances. Gordon Yoder is assaulted. Outsiders swell mob to 2,000.

7:25 P.M., Highway patrol leaves campus. Five minutes later Barnett goes on the radio and announces Meredith is on campus, and says, "we are now completely surrounded by armed forces and we are physically overpowered."

8:00 P.M., President Kennedy delivers a televised speech urging students to obey the law even if they disagree with it; meanwhile, marshals fire tear gas into the mob. Most of the state patrol has returned.

9:00 P.M., Agence France-Press reporter Paul Guihard is murdered.

10:00 P.M., Oxford's Mississippi National Guard company is ordered to reinforce the U.S. Marshals. Snipers in trees start firing and crowd swells to 3,000, most are non-students.

11 P.M. Bystander Ray Gunter is killed.

October 1:

2:15 A.M.: The first U.S. Army military police arrive at the Lyceum. With fixed bayonets they drive rioters off the campus.

6:15 A.M.: General Charles Billingslea declares the campus area secure.

8:15 A.M.: James Meredith is registered and attends his first class, signaling the beginning of the end of segregation in state colleges and universities in Mississippi. Military police accompany him on campus until graduation.

AUGUST 18, 1963: James Meredith graduates from the University of Mississippi with a bachelor's degree in political science.

1962 RIOT SKETCH BY CURTIS WILKIE

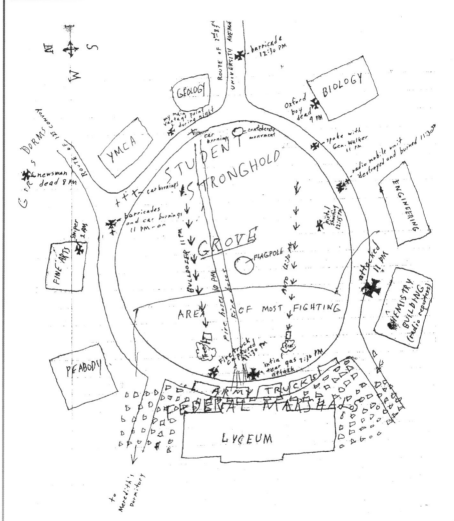

Ole Miss journalism student Curtis Wilkie drew this map the morning after the riot. It shows the riot area near the Lyceum, referring to The Circle as the "Grove." The sketch reveals positions of student demonstrators and federal marshals and notes the approximate locations of where the bodies of French reporter Paul Guihard and bystander Ray Gunter were found. (Curtis Wilkie Collection, Special Collections, University of Mississippi Libraries)

THAT NIGHT AT OLE MISS

By Bob Schieffer

I set foot for the first time on the Ole Miss campus several hours after James Meredith did, and it was one of the most terrifying nights in my life including the days I would later spend in Vietnam.

Danger is expected when you go to a war zone but I had no idea what to expect when I suddenly realized I had been caught between federal marshals and a drunken mob trying to storm the Lyceum building which housed the school registrar's office.

I had just completed three years in the Air Force (where I had never heard a shot fired in anger). I knew little about Ole Miss and less about Meredith. Nor did I appreciate the growing intensity of the civil rights movement that was building across the South. Although I had grown up in the Jim Crow Sunbelt, I missed most of the early days of the civil rights story. The Freedom Rides had begun in 1961; but they happened a long way from the West Coast air bases where I

1

had been stationed and where our attention was focused more on the growing possibility of nuclear war with the Soviet Union.

While I waited for a job opening at my hometown newspaper, the Fort Worth Star-Telegram, I went back to work at the small radio station where I had worked fulltime my last two years in college.

No one was more surprised than I when news director Roy Eaton told me to drive one of the station's "mobile units," to Oxford, Mississippi. We already had one reporter, Bruce Neal, on the scene, and Roy wanted me to back him up. Roy thought the Ole Miss story would be of interest to listeners in the Fort Worth-Dallas area because a right wing rabble-rouser from Dallas, retired Army General Edwin Walker, was trying to organize a force of volunteers to turn Meredith back.

In truth I had no idea what to expect at Ole Miss, but I got a few clues during my all night drive from Fort Worth. Radio waves were filled with stories about General Walker, who was telling his listeners they had been "pushed around too long by the anti-Christ Supreme Court" and urging them to bring "your flag, your tent and your skillet." I hadn't been a reporter long, but I knew enough to realize he wasn't talking about a camping trip.

Even so, I was surprised when I finally drove into Oxford and my panel truck was bombarded with rocks and bottles by gangs of hooligans who lined the streets. I was quickly disabused of the notion that the crowd might mistakenly think I was sympathetic because our station trademark, "The Station that Pioneered Scene Coverage in the Great Southwest" was emblazoned on my truck. This crowd was not impressed. They wanted no part of anyone they didn't know. To them all visitors and reporters were outsiders and were not wanted. For the most part they seemed to be too old to be students, were angry and apparently drunk. I finally got through them, found a place to park the truck, made my way onto the campus and located my colleague, Bruce. As I look back, the next twelve hours were the most terror-filled in a long life of covering not only Vietnam but countless protests that turned violent during the worst Vietnam demonstrations in Washington.

What happened that night is now well known: some 300 federal marshals armed with tear gas fought a pitched battle with protestors armed with rocks and Molotov cocktails, gasoline filled bottles that exploded on impact. Cars were burned, reporters were beaten and without warning a sniper with a rifle opened fire from a rooftop on the crowd below.

During one bizarre episode protestors managed to start a bulldozer that had been left parked nearby by a campus maintenance crew. They aimed the dozer at the marshals then jumped off. Luckily the machine stalled before it reached the marshals.

I was carrying a suitcase size recorder and got knocked down at one point. Bruce and I were jostled several times. Protestors grabbed Dallas-based cameraman Gordon Yoder, whom we both knew, and set his truck afire. We got pushed down by the same crowd but they soon lost interest after smashing my tape recorder and moved on to other targets. Then the sniper opened fire. We hit the dirt. We didn't know where the shots were coming from or who the targets were, but we could hear bullets whistling overhead.

Bruce and I were lucky that night. Many others were not. Before it was over 79 federal marshals were injured, one of them shot through the neck by the sniper. At least forty soldiers were also hurt and two men died, one of them the New York-based Agence France-Presse reporter Paul Guihard, who had been sent to Oxford on his day off because a colleague was on vacation. Also killed was juke-box repair-man Ray Gunter, who had wandered into the riot area to see what the noise was all about.

Bruce and I left the campus early that morning to phone in our reports. When we returned more than 14,000 federal troops had restored order. What we saw that morning looked like the morning after of a World War Two battle.

Several hours later I got my first look at Meredith when his Army security detail surrounded him as he walked toward the Lyceum Building. I was struck by how neatly dressed he was in contrast to those who had been on campus. One wire service reporter was wearing a straw hat and a seersucker blazer, but somehow he had lost his shirt.

Once Meredith was enrolled in class, the story was over for me. I returned to Fort Worth where I was hired as a night police reporter at the Star-Telegram. Over the years, I kept up with some of those who were at Ole Miss that night and in 2003, when I wrote my memoir *This Just In*, I discovered that Henry Gallagher, a Washington lawyer and the young lieutenant who headed up Meredith's security detail, had cleared up a mystery I had always wondered about: Why had it taken federal troops so long to get to the campus that fateful day? In his memoir *A Soldier's Story*, Gallagher described the confusion of his deployment. His New Jersey Military Police unit had been flown to Memphis, and when the 100-unit military vehicle convoy was told to move out for Oxford, they had a problem. They didn't know where it was until they stopped at a roadside gas station and bought a map.

It had been equally confusing in Washington. William Geoghegan, a young Justice Department lawyer who had been left to man Attorney General Robert Kennedy's phone at the Justice Department when Kennedy moved his command center to the White House, said it was total bedlam—no one knew what was happening.

When the President went on national television to make a statement about Meredith's enrollment, he called for calm, unaware that a campus riot was already well underway.

But Meredith remained in school, never out of sight of Gallagher's military security team, and his graduation would be one of the important milestones in the civil rights struggle. Many African-Americans would follow him as a student there.

More than four decades would pass before I returned to the Ole Miss campus in 2008 to cover the presidential debate between Republican John McCain and Barack Obama, who would win the debate and go on to be our first African-American president.

The morning of the debate, my CBS News Colleague Kaylee Hartung and I walked to the campus. There were no traces of the battle that had been fought the night before Meredith enrolled but a bronze statue of his likeness had been erected not far from where the debate was being held.

Also, not far from where Governor Ross Barnett had vowed that no black person would ever attend Ole Miss, I encountered then-Governor Haley Barbour helping students arrange chairs for the debate.

"Governor," I said, "What are you doing here?"

"We just want to make this perfect," he told me.

And it was.

We've still got a ways to go to heal America's racial divide but that day in Oxford I realized how far we have come.

There have been many heroes in this long struggle, and Kathleen Wickham gives well-deserved credit to twelve men and women who risked their lives to tell the story.

This book tells us how they did it.

INTRODUCTION

Agence France-Presse reporter Paul Guihard, the only reporter killed during the civil rights era (1954-1965), was murdered on the campus of the University of Mississippi during the 1962 riot protesting James Meredith's enrollment. His death remains unsolved.

His murder came about because the state's political, economic and religious leaders abdicated their leadership responsibilities by allowing their segregationist views to control their reaction to federal court orders directing the university to enroll its first African-American student. The resulting riot on the bucolic campus was inevitable once Gov. Ross Barnett began rattling the disproved legal argument of interposition.[1] The theory claimed that an individual state has a Constitutional right to nullify or disregard the nation's laws it views as unconstitutional, in this case the 1954 U.S. Supreme Court *Brown v. Board of Education of Topeka* ruling calling for the integration of the nation's public schools.[2]

Much of the South, and in particular Mississippi, wanted nothing more than to be left alone, while still licking its wounds after losing the Civil War a century earlier. Its disparagement of black citizens was complete, including the denial of voting rights, the adoption of Jim Crow laws mandating segregation in public spaces and the construction of a society based on the concept of "separate and equal." It was never equal, of course, but to the state's white citizens interested in maintaining social, economic and political control equal was related to ability, and in their eyes blacks lacked the ability to do much of anything, including enrolling in the state's flagship university.

Jean Lagrange, U.S. bureau chief for AFP, said on learning of Guihard's death that he "died in the achievement of his journalistic mission such as he conceived it: on the same ground of the action. He knew the risks that are of the first lines."[3] According to Lagrange his colleague flew to Mississippi "with a calm courage and with a profound sense of responsibility."[4] He was doing his job, which was to report the story so that the public would be informed of the actions of government so that citizens could come to their own decisions regarding the rightness or wrongness of the actions reported.

And so it was also for the 300-plus newsmen and women representing newspapers, magazines, radio and television in the U.S., Canada and Europe, who came to document the enrollment of the first African-American in any "white" public school in Mississippi. For despite the subsequent 1955 Supreme Court ruling urging desegregation proceed with "all deliberate speed"[5] not a single black student had crossed the color barrier. In the end, the journalists went away with the personal satisfaction of knowing that they did not waver when bricks and bullets were flying, that they scoured the campus and town for viewpoints and they did their job of informing the public of the story in Oxford.

Upon joining the journalism faculty at the University of Mississippi in 1999, I went looking for the site where Guihard's body was found. The location is near a meditation circle between Bryant Hall and the Student Union. One of my kind, a journalist, had been killed and his death had become a historical footnote. In an all too real sense Guihard had been left behind. Where was the outrage? Where was a sustained call for an open investigation?

The pressroom in the Lyceum during the integration crisis.
Photo by Ed Meek.

I was a young reporter in New Jersey in 1976 when Don Bolles, an investigative reporter for *The Arizona Republic*, was murdered in what was originally believed to be a mob hit but later found to be the work of a wealthy land developer.

Bob Greene of Newsday launched a campaign, not only to find who killed Bolles, but also to complete the reporting he'd begun. Some 40 reporters and editors from 23 newspapers reporters gave up vacation time, took sabbaticals and quit their jobs to help investigate. I had no vacation time that year and regrettably was unable to go to Arizona. The reporters' outrage stayed with me.

Why was there not an equally determined effort to solve Guihard's murder? An obituary in *The New York Times*, a half-hearted investigation by local authorities, a private burial in France—that's all? Make no mistake, Guihard was murdered. He was shot in the back from a foot away.[6] To me, the murder of a journalist is akin to shooting a bullet through the First Amendment because those who seek to stifle the press are dangerously close to imposing mob rule on society. Limiting the media is an affront to democracy and the public's right to know about the actions of government and institutions with power over public affairs.

The press has faced such challenges throughout its existence. Throughout the tense years of the civil rights era, reporters were shot at, beaten, threatened, and challenged in pursuit of the public's right to know what was happening in their communities. According to United Press International reporter John Herbers, "the threat of being mauled" by segregationists was just one of many problems reporters faced in Mississippi and other Deep South states where white supremacists ruled with an iron hand.[7] The best known are NBC reporter Richard Valeriani, who was beaten in Selma, and *Birmingham News* photographer Tom Langston, who was assaulted in Birmingham. Claude Sitton famously said when threatened by a mob, "If you shoot me, *The New York Times* will have fifteen reporters in here tomorrow morning."[8]

To many white Mississippians, the Civil War was still a vivid memory passed on by ancestors who had served in the Confederate army and whose portraits hung in family homes. Gov. Barnett's grandfather, for example, had fought in the Civil War. As University Chancellor J.D. Williams noted: "A defeated and pillaged people do not easily forget. The bitterness of that defeat was burned into our memory by the savage rule, imposed from without, of the Reconstruction Era. Jealousy and a certain distrust of the federal government exist throughout this country. It is an established fact of political life in Mississippi and in the rest of the Deep South."[9]

Reporters interviewing James Meredith on his first day of classes. Photo by Ed Meek.

Southerners responded with massive resistance to demands that they change their way of life. Fueled by belief in "the 'Southern Way of Life,' the social pattern of the complete separation of the races,"[10] Barnett raged against Meredith's enrollment in his speeches and in newspaper stories and on the airwaves. The state's political leadership responded with massive resistance battling Meredith in federal court and plotting how to prevent him from enrolling over an 18-month period.

The state's white citizens had quickly joined the newly formed Citizen's Council after the Brown decision and saw no reason to given up their opposition to integration in light of federal intervention in the Meredith case. As Williams noted: "not even the bloodiest war in our history and the century since has changed in its essentials... No other way of life appears acceptable."[11]

And while opposition to Meredith's enrollment roiled across the state, few voices were raised in alarm as the state's political leadership abdicated its responsibilities. And those that did were either ostracized, viewed with amusement or dismissed as outliners.

Reporters on the steps of the Lyceum prior to the arrival of the U.S. Marshal.s Photo by Ed Meek.

Oxford author William Faulkner, the state's literary giant having won both the Noble Prize and the Pulitzer Prize, was subtle. He dealt with race issues in his novels as commentary on relationships between whites and blacks over time without taking a firm stance on either side of the question. Historian Shelby Foote said Faulkner noted before his death that summer that the outcome of the Meredith case rested on common sense. "The white people," Faulkner said, "have already lost their heads; it depends on whether the Negroes can keep theirs."[12] His meaning was ambiguous.

James Meredith, the loner who began his quest to enroll in The University of Mississippi without the backing of a national organization, recognized that the world was changing. He experienced discrimination during his Air Force service and was appalled by the way American soldiers treated the Japanese during his tenure there. At the same time, across the globe, colonial rule was being rejected, most notably in India, Algeria, Cyprus and Africa. Black Americans, profoundly impacted by these democratic movements abroad and their service during World War II, wanted the same opportunities at home. They pressed for social change and civil rights and brought their voices to the nation's attention with demands for equal treatment, especially through restaurant sit-ins and, famously, the year-long Montgomery bus protest.

The reporters who streamed into Mississippi to cover the Meredith integration crisis came from large and small newspapers, national magazines, news networks and foreign news organizations. Some had previously written about the push for black civil rights. Others had not. They were young, determined and committed to journalism. What happened to them at Ole Miss is a window into the psychologies that draw people to journalism and an examination of how journalists practice their craft under fire.[13] They left the familiarity of their newsrooms, walked into a maelstrom, emerged with injuries, and left with a changed perspective about their profession and a different view about America's role in the world.

The 300-plus reporters assigned to Oxford did not go to Mississippi to judge. They were there to report objectively. There would be no personal opinion in their dispatches, no sensationalism, no subtle analysis, no personal agendas, no taking sides in the black struggle for civil rights. All, however, relied on the accumulated experience of colleagues covering the desegregation of public and private institutions in both the North and South. For the most part, school integration in cities like Chicago and Detroit had been resolved without the deep rancor that occurred across the Deep South.[14] Now they had arrived in the Magnolia State ahead of breaking news.

A southern governor had drawn a line in the sand and dared the federal government to cross it. Barnett was a small town lawyer and first-term governor who won election on a segregation plank. His position on state's rights and opposition to segregation evoked comparisons to the Civil War. Not even Gov. Orval Faubus in Little Rock in 1957 went as far as Barnett in ignoring federal integration orders. And while the U.S. Army was called out in Arkansas, its task was ensure the enrollment of the nine students chosen to integrate the high school.

From the moment the reporters set foot in Mississippi, coverage of the Ole Miss crisis presented challenges unlike any they had encountered. Oxford, a small rural town of fewer than 5,000 residents, was located some 70 miles southeast of Memphis. While there was a small commercial airport, there were insufficient hotel rooms for a few dozen journalists, much less 300, and few long-distance telephone lines to transmit their stories.

Reporter Richard Starnes, writing for the Scripps Howard Newspaper Alliance, observed that closing the university, mentioned as a possibility by state officials, would put a dent in the region's well-being, if not reason for being.[15] One businessman told a reporter for *Newsday* he would see his business drop 75 percent if the university closed.[16]

Confronted with local opposition, they found themselves in a Mississippi maze. It was not their turf and the topic was contentious. Press badges from northern newspapers were their only armor. Avoiding tear gas while changing film or jotting down facts, they called in their stories, tended to their wounds and returned to campus to record history being made.

Guihard's story is reflected here in the recollections and experiences of twelve of his peers assigned to the Ole Miss story, any one of whom could have met the same fate. Facing the very real possibility of being killed, each made the choice to seek the truth despite the risks. This book reflects my quest to bring Guihard's murder to the public's attention, hoping that, in some way, it might be solved, and to pay tribute to the reporters who came to Oxford without fear for their safety and with the commitment to share the Ole Miss story with the public.

My quest has taken me to archives and libraries throughout the South and East and to France where Paul's brother, Alain Guihard, graciously met me in St. Malo, introduced me to his brother's childhood friends, showed me where they lived as boys and were his brother to school. He brought Paul to life as only a brother can by his memories of swimming on the Brittany beaches, walking home from school for lunch and surviving under Nazi occupation when food and clothing was scarce and safety was a constant concern.

For the dozen reporters profiled here, their stories serve a similar purpose. Many of the reporters viewed covering the Ole Miss story as the most significant story of their careers. Time has not shaded their memories of their time in Oxford. They recall the campus, the town, the restaurants where they ate and the hotels where they lived with unusual clarity, considering how many more stories they have written and places they have visited over the past 55 years. Thus, this book weaves their stories through a common narrative: that of covering a riot where a newsman was murdered and reporters were attacked and their commitment to the public to get the story no matter the danger was tested.

Readers and viewers are linked to their names and faces through a para-social construct that supports the role of journalists as chroniclers of change.[17] In my media ethics classes, I teach my students that the primary stakeholder in any story is the public. These reporters honored that value with their lives and, in the process, learned a lot about their own tenacity, abilities and relationships with their readers and viewers. These men and woman were simply among the best journalists of their generation. Profiled are 12 American reporters, including two women and two African Americans, a fledging reporter who gained national notoriety, and another best known for his photographs of Muhammed Ali. In addition, a chapter is devoted to Paul Guihard, of Agence French-Presse.

CBS anchor Dan Rather made his debut on national television in covering the integration crisis. Richard Valeriani, reporting for NBC radio and television, called in radio reports on the hour and filmed broadcast stand-ups in between.

Claude Sitton, whom CBS reporter Dan Rather called "a great vacuum sweeper reporter with *The New York Times* (who) had pioneered the kind of constant day-by-day front-page story of the civil rights movement when very few other people in print would do it" is prominently included here, and for that very reason.[18]

Karl Fleming of *Newsweek*, often Sitton's sidekick when they were the only reporters present, was a staple of news magazine journalism, while Flip Schulke, a freelance photographer for *Life*, was equally notable for his photography. Schulke may have been the last person to speak to Guihard.

The danger came close to being fatal for Gordon Yoder, a broadcast photographer from Dallas, who, with his wife, barely escaped after the mob attacked their station wagon. Fred Powledge of *The*

The author with Alain Guihard.
Photo by Marie Gerard.

Atlanta Journal survived three beatings, narrowly escaping the same fate as Guihard.

On orders from her editor, Dorothy Gilliam, the first African-American woman hired by *The Washington Post*, was kept away from Oxford for a week. Gilliam's task when she arrived was to capture the mood of the African-American community, a story overlooked in the drama surrounding Meredith.

Moses Newson of the Baltimore *Afro-American* arrived in Oxford September 30, drawn to Mississippi by his pal, Jimmy Hicks of New York's *Amsterdam News*. Yet neither was allowed on campus. While the black press was kept at arm's length, it was not silent.

The mood of the community intrigued *Newsday*'s Michael Dorman, who tracked down William Faulkner's brother, John, seeking his opinion. Faulkner had died just three months earlier leaving a void in his native Oxford. Neal Gregory of *The (Memphis) Commercial Appeal* reported on sermons asking congregations in churches for acceptance and repentance.[19]

Sidna Brower, editor of the student newspaper, *The Mississippian*, was the reporter left behind when the others moved on to the next big story. For her, the story did not end in October. She was reviled and spit upon by fellow students and called to task by state officials, but she was also honored with a Pulitzer nomination.

Whereas many Mississippi newspapers and television and radio stations distorted the news and allowed segregationist beliefs to cloud their obligation as journalists, a small group of courageous Mississippi reporters were notable for their commitment to the truth: Hazel Brannon Smith, publisher of the *Lexington Advertiser*; Hodding Carter III, editor and publisher of the *Greenville Delta Democrat-Times*; Ira Harkey, publisher of the *Pasagoula Chronicle*, Bill Minor, Mississippi columnist for the *New Orleans Times-Picayune*; and Lucy Komisar, editor of the *Mississippi Free Press*. Their contributions are acknowledged in an Afterword.

Photo of Paul Guihard courtesy of Alain Guihard.

PAUL GUIHARD

Agence French-Presse reporter Paul Guihard was looking forward to enjoying his weekend in New York City when his editor sent him to cover the Mississippi integration crisis. Normally a copy editor, Guihard was given the assignment because the bureau was short-staffed. His editor, Jean Lagrange, recalled that Guihard was excited by the assignment because it took him away from the predictability of the copy desk.[20]

He would return to New York in a coffin, the only reporter killed during the civil rights era. Lagrange would write in a memorial: "The offices of the AFP in the United States saw the brutal disappearance of one who they could count on in all circumstances.

Paul was a friend to all. His sense of humor, his natural generosity, added to his professional qualities."[21]

Though theories abound, Paul's murder remains a mystery.[22] His case is listed by the FBI as unsolved. Evan Thomas, in his biography of Robert F. Kennedy, speculates that Guihard, seeing men unloading weapons near the Ward Dormitory, aimed his camera at them, and was shot in the back.[23] Though Guihard was not a news photographer, his brother, Alain, of Lyon, France, said Paul habitually carried a small camera. A former Ole Miss coed at the scene partially corroborates Thomas's theory. She claims to have seen a man leaning over Guihard's body and smashing a camera into the ground. She, however, didn't witness the shooting.

Guihard's partial hearing loss in his left ear might also have been a factor. According to his brother, Alain, if danger came from his left side, he would have been slow to respond.[24] Another theory involves an alleged dispute between a segregationist and another French reporter earlier in the day at the Robert E. Lee Hotel in Jackson. He was about Paul's height and had a red beard. This segregationist may have trailed Guihard to Oxford thinking he was the other reporter.

An unidentified man dressed in white has also been named as a possible suspect.[25] This possible assailant mentioned in FBI files was described as a sailor, or a kitchen worker.[26] The Lafayette County sheriff blamed the killing on U.S. marshals.[27] But no man, or group, was ever positively identified as the killer. The fact that Guihard was shot in the back from a foot away meant the shooting was deliberate, not the result of random gunfire.

Guihard moved without fear toward the chaos. As a young boy, living in St. Malo, France, under German occupation during World War II, he became

Paul Guihard in the British Army.
Courtesy of Alain Guihard.

adept at navigating streets filled with enemy soldiers. Because of his dual citizenship, he served in the British army in Cyprus where he saw street fighting and learned how to take precautions.

Guihard began his last day on a flight from New York to Jackson. Photographer Sammy Schulman, who worked for AFP as head of photo operations after a long and distinguished career with International News Service, accompanied him.[28]

Schulman, 56, had photographed the 1938-1940 Finnish-Russian War, and then Sicily, Salerno, and French Morocco in World War II.[29] He was the only news photographer present when President Franklin D. Roosevelt met with British Prime Minister Winston Churchill and French General Charles de Gaulle in Casablanca in 1943 under wartime secrecy.[30]

The men complemented each other. Schulman was a scrappy New Yorker with a British wife who could land in almost any city, in the midst of any crisis, and come out with the definitive news photograph.[31] Guihard was a foreign newsman whose international view of events had been shaped by his youthful experiences living in St. Malo, France, during World War II. They were neither part of the story nor isolated from its greater implications.

As Guihard and Schulman boarded the plane in New York, Guihard shrugged off warnings from colleagues who had faced thuggish law enforcement officials in the South when blacks demonstrated at lunch counters and bus stations. Guihard was blasé: "I'm going to pose as a Kentucky colonel and cover this thing with a mint julep in my hand."[32]

During the flight to Jackson an airline stewardess, inquiring about his business in Mississippi, remarked, "Oh, I know, you're going down to the nigger thing."[33] Guihard turned to Schulman and speaking French said: "These people. It'll take them a hundred years to start forgetting."[34]

On arriving in Jackson, Guihard and Schulman rented a white Chevrolet and drove to the governor's mansion.[35] More than 3,000 people had assembled at a rally sponsored by the White Citizens Council.[36]

Two months after the 1954 *Brown v. Board of Education* ruling banning school segregation, the Citizens Council organization was founded in Indianola, Mississippi, in the heart of the Mississippi Delta. Chapters were formed across the South, and the orga-

Gov. Ross Barnett, photo by Ed Meek, courtesy University of Mississippi Archives

nization was often viewed as an upper-class version of the Ku Klux Klan. Citizen Council members were typically drawn from community leaders, who used economic pressure, the media, and promotional materials to advocate their views. Gov. Barnett's political base could be found among the membership lists of the Citizens Council.[37]

At 11 a.m. that morning, Barnett released a statement to the press: "My friends, I repeat to the people of Mississippi now, I will never yield a single inch in my determination to win the fight we are engaged in. I call upon every Mississippian to keep his faith and his courage. We will never surrender."[38] This message, broadcast over WLBT-TV in the state capital of Jackson, attracted the attention of segregationists throughout the viewing area.

The governor's message was a call to action. Packing weapons and Confederate flags, rednecks, students from area colleges, and troublemakers from all over the South headed to Oxford. Their goal was to save Mississippi, to fight against change, and to preserve the citadel of learning known as "Ole Miss" (slave term for the master's mother or grandmother on plantations).

The scene was set for a violent confrontation.

Meanwhile, after the rally, Guihard walked into the Citizens Council's offices and interviewed Executive Director Louis Hollis. Guihard was a warm, friendly person and people were comfortable with him, sharing information and coffee. As a result he received permission to file his last story from Hollis' office. Hollis subsequently viewed Guihard as a friend, sympathetic to the council's opposition to Meredith's enrollment.[39] Guihard's appearance in the council office took on new meaning after his death when segregationists claimed that Guihard was "one of them" and that a federal marshal had been responsible for his death.[40] Neither claim was ever substantiated. Guihard was just a reporter looking for a phone.

Then, it was late afternoon and time to head to Oxford, a trip that would take almost four hours. As Guihard and Schulman drove north, they listened to President John F. Kennedy's 8 p.m. speech on the radio. The broadcast included the news that Meredith had arrived in Oxford and that the atmosphere on campus was calm. Unbeknownst to Kennedy, moments before he went on the air the order to fire tear gas had been given, setting off a full-scale riot. Kennedy, in his prepared speech, reminded listeners: "In a government of laws and not of men, no man, however prominent or powerful—and no mob, however unruly or boisterous—is entitled to defy a court of law."[41]

"Oh hell, the story's over," Guihard said to Schulman in the car." But we might as well go and clean it up."[42] A Mississippi Highway patrolman stopped Guihard's car as it approached the campus at around 8:40 p.m. The officer warned the pair, "I can't guarantee your life or property if you drive in.[43] Guihard acknowledged the officer's warning and drove onto the campus toward the Confederate statue dedicated to university students who fought in the Civil War. There were no barriers, and people were coming and going.

The pair parked and walked toward the crowd of angry students and outsiders. Night had fallen. The grounds were dark and the stench of tear gas was in the air. The roar of the mob rolled across campus.

As Guihard and Schulman moved through the campus, they encountered dark figures darting back and forth. Photographers were advising each other to "shoot and run." The flash bulbs gave them away, and the mob attacked them and smashed their cameras.

Guihard and Schulman decided to split up. It was both a newsman's tactic and a military maneuver. They had different but complementary duties that night and by splitting up more ground could be covered. At the same time a reporter doesn't necessarily walk into chaos but flanks the scene and observes without barreling through the crowd. Guihard told Schulman, "I'll see what's doing and see you back here at the car in an hour, then."[44]

Less than ten minutes later he was shot in the back from one foot away, the bullet tearing into his heart.[45] His body was found by students in a dark area of campus near a women's dormitory. The location was out of sight of the federal officials protecting the campus.[46]

An experienced reporter like Guihard knew the risks involved in street reporting. Tensions are often high. Protagonists face off against antagonists. But he didn't say, "I can't go there, that's too dangerous." It was his job to get the story. As a journalist he was committed the moment he accepted the assignment. It's almost like taking holy orders. He doubtless thought to himself, "I'm going to go forward even if it is a mob." He could seek a safer path by circling the action, taking shelter if gunfire erupted, but he could not cover the riot from inside a newsroom. He could keep an eye out for fellow reporters stationed in the Circle, the 3.5-acre green space in front of the Lyceum where the riot was underway, and from them learn what was happening. Various people said they thought they saw Guihard in the tear gas smog, or perhaps spoke to him as he ambled across the greenspace. But then he disappeared in the miasmas.

It is said that some people are born to be musicians, writers, or artists—that creative souls are born, not made, and that youthful interests do not translate into a career without the influence of others.

St. Malo, France
Photo by Kathleen Wickham

Paul and younger brother Alain.
Photo courtesy of Alain Guihard.

Paul's influences were war-torn France, where print and radio news was censored and propaganda was the norm.

Their parents had sent them to live with their grandparents in St. Malo, France, during the early days of the London Blitz. Their mother Betty Crowther, who was born in Yorkshire, met his French-born father while working at a hotel in the Guernsey Islands. They spent the war years managing the hotel they owned in London. Alain was just an infant at the time and Paul was seven years older. They would not see their parents again until the war ended in 1945.

For the young boys life on the Brittany coast was a lonely, wistful existence marked by shortages of food, clothing and school supplies. Their clothes became tattered rags yet were worn until they were long outgrown. The boys and their grandparents were evacuated inland when, after D-Day, the Allied bombs rained down, destroying most of St. Malo. Their beach playground, the Plage de Bon Secours, with its saltwater pool became a minefield, while the medieval walled citadel with its labyrinthic network of cobbled streets and ramparts sheltering massive granite buildings was almost totally destroyed. The steeple on the Roman Catholic Cathedral of St. Vincent suffered the indignity of collapsing inside the structure under the Allied shelling. Adventure surrounded the boys too, in the history of St. Malo. In the 17th and 18th centuries France granted St. Malo's sailor merchants, known as corsairs, license to act as pirates, "coursing" after enemy ships and earning a portion of the proceeds.[47]

Alain Guihard said his brother Paul "couldn't resist reading a newspaper from beginning to end," as if he had to consume all the day's news in one sitting. [48] It is easy to see how from the ramparts of the walled medieval old city fronting the beach a boy missing his parents could imagine he could see England across the channel, and with the information pulled from a newspaper, living in an occupied country and knowing of the history of St. Malo want to explore the world through the power of journalism.

It was this quest for knowledge, the curiosity to know the truth and the desire to create understanding that propelled Paul into the morass.

Guihard became a full-time AFP staffer in 1953 after returning from the British military service. He spent a year in Paris at its English-speaking news desk before he was transferred to New York in 1960. He covered a variety of assignments including a flood disaster in Honduras and the developing Cuban missile crisis. While in New York he also freelanced for the *Daily Sketch* of London.[49] At the time of her son's death, his mother observed that Paul had "wanted to be in newspapers since boyhood. He never wanted to do anything else."[50]

To the Rev. Michel Leutellier, who grew up with Guihard in St. Malo, it was no surprise Paul became a writer and journalist. Leutellier recalled that Paul could be found at lunch writing in his tablet. Though some of his teachers disapproved of his satirical writings, he edited a school journal called *The Lame Duck*. He produced two editions of about thirty pages each, with contributions from about ten other students. "When he wrote, it was pure French and very pleasant. He had a lot of ideas and he knew how to present his ideas in a very original way."[51]

Leutellier recalled, "We were boys together and then young men. We discussed different things from boyish matters. We talked about philosophy, history, politics, etc. He was very interesting for me because in the seminary and even at school [we had not] this widening of the mind he could have [learned] in a journalism school."[52]

Leutellier, who went on to become a parish priest, said he kept in contact with Guihard over the years and followed his journalism career from afar, observing he was always taking risks in his work. "I was doing my military service, and I was going to Senegal; so I got in touch with Paul before leaving. He saw me in uniform, and when leaving the house, he said, 'If you were in the British army, we would give you two weeks in the military jail. You're all buttoned down, but your shoes are not shiny.' I remember we laughed, but I think the British army was not very kind with its soldiers."[53]

According to Leutellier, Paul was a loner who walked home for lunch to his grandparents' home in St. Servan, a suburb of St. Malo. He was one of the "privileged" class of students whose family could afford tuition. His clothes, purchased in England had a different cut and style than those worn by his schoolmates. "In those days, that was a big difference," Leutellier said.

Today, Paul's elementary school, run by the Christian Brothers, is little changed. Classrooms surround a playground where Leutellier recalled spending recess with Paul during the German occupation. It takes only a little imagination to think of the games Paul played while working on his satirical cartoons and stories—the defeat of the Nazis, France's victory over tyranny, life in London with his parents, the future.

At 17, he covered the 1948 London Olympic Games for Agence France-Presse. Nearly fourteen years later his life ended at the University of Mississippi. *Life* magazine photographer Flip Schulke, who may have been the last newsman to speak to him, watched Guihard heading up a street toward the Lyceum. "I yelled, you know, *get down!* And this French accent came back at me, saying, 'I'm not worried, I was in Cyprus.'"[54]

As Schulke huddled under the shrubbery, Guihard disappeared into the tear gas behind the Fine Arts building. *New York Herald-Tribune* reporter Robert S. Bird's description of covering the riot provides a playbook for how Guihard probably faced the danger that led to his death. Bird wrote:

> A reporter doesn't exactly cover a riot of that kind in the con-
> ventional sense—with pen and pad in hand, I mean. You uncap
> your ballpoint and hold it in your trouser pocket to jab into the

eye of the first maniac who tries to slug you. You slip your notepa-
per into a rear pocket in case you need it to wipe the blood away.

You don't rush into a riot. You sidle up to it warily and allow
yourself to be sucked into it. For it is already out of control and
has its own brainless system of dynamics. You understand full
well that you personally, as a news reporter, are a prime target
for the mob if your identity is discovered. You're scared to death,
but there's no time to think about that. Suddenly you are right
in the middle of it all and you must now deal with the immediate
action swirling in a 20-foot radius.[55]

Into that swirl Guihard vanished.

Unlike other members of the press corps, who had arrived on
campus days before and were issued press passes, Guihard, due to
his late arrival, carried no such identification. He also was unknown
to the press corps. What made him stand out were his stature, his red
beard and his accent. Schulke said, "I always remembered [Guihard's
statement] because I didn't know much about Cyprus, but [Ole Miss]
was a dangerous place."[56]

Schulke, underscoring Bird's observations about how a journalist proceeds into a riot, but speaking as a photographer, said, "The
camera is like a wall between you and danger, and you take chances.
I had never been under fire before. You wonder if it's worth it... I
reached a point where I decided that if I was going to risk my life, it
had to be for something I truly, deeply believed in."[57]

Gunshots rang out repeatedly that night. Another man, Ray Gunter,
was killed standing near the Hilgard railroad bridge at the university's main entrance. Gunter was from Abbeville, a dozen or so miles
north of Oxford. A jukebox repairman, he came to see what all the
fuss was about. His first child was born nine days later. His assailant
also was never identified.

The U.S. marshals were told to not fire their weapons and did not,
except in rare instances.[58] For Robert Kennedy, who as attorney general was charged with seeing that federal laws were enforced, the
decision not to return fire was painful. As Evan Thomas wrote: "Say
no to defensive fire and [Kennedy] risked sacrificing his men, several

Tear gas explosions in the Circle.
Photo by Ed Meek.

of them dear friends, and letting the mob string up Meredith from one of the gracious oaks in the Grove. Say yes and he risked provoking a second Civil War."[59]

As Guihard headed toward the Circle, the mob surged in his direction. Schulman veered in another direction, skirting the 10-acre Grove, a hallowed ground presently used for tailgating before football games. A student told him to hide his cameras as "some bums up there (near the Lyceum) are smashing them."[60]

It is not known if Guihard ever made it as far as the Circle. His body was found at the southeast corner of the Ward Dormitory, about 12 feet east of the building's wall and about 55 yards from Grove Loop Street, also east of the dormitory.[61]

To Meredith, an Air Force veteran, Guihard was simply a casualty of an armed conflict. When asked recently for his reaction to Guihard's death he remained noncommittal: "What soldiers do is kill enemies. If there was any real surprise to me, it was that only two people got killed."[62]

Students walking in the area near the Fine Arts building found his body around 9 p.m.[63] Education major Hugh Calvin Murray of Meadville, Mississippi, told FBI investigators a female student stopped him while he was walking in front of Ward. She said, "Oh look!" and pointed toward the east end of the building. Murray said he observed "a man lying on his back with his feet extended out onto the sidewalk."[64] The site was near a clump of bushes in an unlit area.[65]

Johann W. Rush, a freelance photographer from Jackson working as a stringer for CBS, said some thought that tear gas had felled Guihard.[66] Murray "advised that he assumed that this person had suffered a heart attack. He immediately removed the glasses from this person and began massaging his heart. He recalled that the victim had a slight pulse beat; however, he did not feel a heartbeat. He estimated that he massaged this person's heart for at least 30 minutes when another person came by, believed to be a student, name unknown, who relieved him, and this person massaged his heart for another 20-30 minutes."[67]

Pharmacy student Tom Brown of Jackson, Mississippi, said when he arrived about a half dozen students were already present, and they had elevated Guihard's feet believing him to be in shock.[68] "I asked if he had any pulse. They said he did. I checked and found no pulse. There was no air escaping through his nostrils or his mouth and his eyes were thoroughly dilated. There was no heartbeat to my knowledge. I put my ear to his chest and could not hear a heartbeat. However, we continued to massage his chest, and we once tried mouth-to-mouth resuscitation. But to no avail. I am sure and was sure at that time that the man was dead," he recalled.[69]

During the time Murray was with Guihard, the victim uttered no sound. Murray estimated that no more than ten individuals came by the area. He recalled that someone, possibly one of the housemothers from a nearby girls' dormitory, brought a blanket and covered Guihard's body.[70]

Murray told the FBI that he was not aware that the man had been shot and could not recall seeing any blood on his brown coat.[71] Brown, however, noted that Guihard had bitten his lip and there was dried blood on his lip.[72]

Cort Best, a photojournalist with the *Courier-Journal* and *Louisville Times* in Kentucky, said that, although he was at the scene shortly after the students discovered Guihard's body, he did not take photographs at the request of a housemother at the scene.[73]

Meanwhile, other people were working on getting help for Guihard. R.J. Bonds, a radio station manager in nearby Batesville, told FBI investigators that he was in the YMCA building near the Confederate statue when a person he assumed was a student came in and asked to use a telephone to call an ambulance.[74] The ambulance, however, could not get through the crowd. Help came from the campus infirmary in the form of a student with a car.[75]

Rush and Brown said they and several other students used the blanket to carry Guihard to the car to take him to the city hospital on Van Buren Avenue.[76] They had to carry him through the Ward dormitory as the car was parked in the rear. Brown said the student with the car arrived about 10 or 15 minutes after he arrived: "A boy rode up in a car—or he walked up, his car was behind the dormitory and said we could put the man in his car and he would take him to the city hospital in Oxford."[77]

Graduate student Donald Lee Dugger of Independence, Missouri, said he was one of the three people who transported Guihard to the hospital. Dugger told the FBI he went to the student infirmary to assist his wife who worked there and was asked to "remove Paul Guihard from Ward Hall to the Oxford Hospital."[78]

Brown recalled that, 10 minutes later, an ambulance arrived and he informed the driver Guihard had already been transported to the hospital.[79]

Murray Sutherland, an ambulance driver for the Douglas Funeral Home, said that he drove to the hospital to determine the man's status after learning Guihard's body had been taken to the hospital: "We learned that he was DOA, that he was a citizen of France, and they would have an inquest."[80]

Mayor Richard Elliott, who owned a funeral home, said he initially learned of Guihard's death when a student stopped him on the Square saying that someone had had a heart attack on campus and a doctor and ambulance were needed.[81] Guihard's body was taken to Memphis for autopsy. It was there it was noted that a bullet had penetrated the back from a foot away.[82]

Schulman learned of Guihard's death while examining the equipment in the photo lab of the student newspaper, *The Mississippian*. Editor Sidna Brower said she was showing Schulman the lab when someone knocked on the door and informed them of Guihard's death. "Oh, my God, that's my guy," Schulman cried.[83] Brower does not recall the time, only that the newspaper had made its darkroom, newsroom and telephones available to the visiting media. The student newspaper was in Brady Hall, near the University Avenue entrance to campus, about a quarter-mile from the Lyceum.

Schulman formally identified Guihard at the funeral home and picked up Guihard's personal effects at the hospital, signing a receipt.[84] Hospital records indicated Guihard was already dead from a gunshot wound when he arrived at the hospital.[85]

The first news report of Guihard's death was stated in a one-sentence telegram sent at 10:59 p.m. to *The News and Courier*, Charleston, S.C., by Anthony Harrigan.[86] Ten minutes later, at 11:09 p.m., Richard Starnes, a reporter for the Scripps-Howard Newspaper Alliance, had Western Union transmit a complete story about the night's events with a paragraph about Guihard's death below the lead.[87]

The White House learned of Guihard's death at 12:30 a.m., October 1, when Jack Rosenthal, a special assistant to the attorney general, called the White House seeking to speak to Assistant Attorney General Burke Marshall or Robert Kennedy. The president's secretary, Evelyn Lincoln, who answered the call, took the message from Rosenthal: "Would you tell him that a reporter for the London *Daily Sketch*, whose name is Paul Guihard, was killed in Oxford just now? His body was found with a bullet in the back, next to a women's dormitory."[88]

The president sent a telegram expressing his condolences to Jean Marin, president and director general of Agence France-Presse in Paris:

> I want to express to you the shock of the American people on the death of your correspondent, Paul Guihard, last night in Oxford, Mississippi. The American people, I am sure, as well as the law-abiding citizens of the state of Mississippi, share my sorrow that this could have happened in our country. I hope you will convey my condolences to his family.[89]

President Kennedy arranged to have an Air Force C-47 plane transport Guihard's body to New York for a memorial service. The service was held October 5 at the French Roman Catholic Church of St. Vincent de Paul on 23rd Street near Sixth Avenue. AFP made the arrangements to fly Guihard's remains to France via Air France. No family members were on the flight, but Alain Guihard met the plane when it landed at Orly Airport in Paris.

Flowers were placed on the spot where Guihard died the next day. Paul Mathias, the American correspondent for *Paris Match*, a French news magazine, conducted his own investigation and came up with no suspects.

Alain Guihard had last seen his brother three years before his death. While completing his military obligation in Algiers, Alain would receive long letters from Paul concerning his ambitions to be a playwright and life in New York. He was still in Algiers when he heard a radio announcement of his brother's death: "His name was given, no possible doubt."[90] Alain was scheduled for discharge within the week and the British Army arranged for him to leave immediately. Alain met Paul's plane and drove to St. Malo.

Their parents learned of Paul's death from AFP's London manager.[91] Alain recalled: "You can imagine the shock to them, but my mother, more than my father, managed to control her emotion, and went on carrying out her usual tasks, without anyone noticing the difference, so she said!"[92]

The death of Guihard stunned his colleagues. Jean Lagrange, U.S. bureau chief for Agence French Presse, wrote a memorial letter published in *The Washington Post:*

> Paul Guihard died in the achievement of his journalistic mission such as he conceived it: on the same ground of the action. He knew the risks that are of the first lines. But he accepted them with a calm courage and with a profound sense of responsibilities; he did not want to describe what he had not visually witnessed, with objectivity and sincerity.
>
> Saturday evening, I spoke to him to develop this report, which was to be, for him, the last.
>
> As always, he was delighted to drop his usually work routine of writing, with his usual enthusiasm, toward a new professional

Paul Guihard.
Courtesy of Alain Guihard.

experience. His name lengthens the too-long list of those who, in their profession, have, like him, been victims of their desire to serve the cause of honest information.

The Agence French-Presse lost a talented colleague. The offices of the AFP in the United States saw the brutal disappearance of one whom they could count on in all circumstances. Paul was a friend to all. His sense of humor, his natural generosity, added to his professional qualities, we will miss now.[93]

In their eulogies, colleagues recalled Guihard's nickname of "Flash," earned because of his passion for journalism.[94] Friends also described the bearded, husky, six-foot tall bachelor as a "bon vivant." Felix Bolo, an AFP editor on duty the day Guihard was killed, wrote in a letter to historian William Doyle, "He had a great sense of humor, English or French, and he always seemed to be happy, kidding and joking all the time. He was a 'force de la nature,' as we say in French. He would have made an excellent movie actor, a natural and huge Rob Roy."[95]

Paul Guihard is buried in the family tomb in St. Malo. AFP sent a representative to the funeral. Leutellier conducted a traditional Catholic burial service. Paul Guihard's family accepted the inevitable and moved on. According to Alain: "My mother dealt with it in the best possible way on the day they learned about it. She went on with her usual work in the hotel. My father took it more dramatically. I think really for both of them it's that sort of event, which stays with you throughout your life. One of the worst things, I think, for parents, is to lose a child. There's nothing worse."[96]

LAST REPORT FROM DEAD NEWSMAN

Agence France-Press, Oct. 1, 1962

It is difficult to believe one is in the very center of the gravest Constitutional crisis that the United States has known since the War of the Secession. One realizes it with a certain terror only at the moment when the mob in the street, suddenly serious, intones "Dixie" the vibrant hymn of the old Confederacy. One has to hear also the shouts when, from the windows, the spokesman of the White Citizens Council proclaims, "Don't let America rejoin Africa," or, further, "A black America will lose its greatness."

It is only in one of those moments that one grasps the gap of a century between Washington and the Southern irredintists.

The Civil War never came to an end. "The South will rise again," proclaim the posters pasted on the walls and on the automobile bumpers. The mob sings and laughs under the hot October sun, and from the first minute one realizes that this mob is completely unconscious of the enormity of its gesture, of its repercussions, and the interest which it excites throughout the whole world.[97]

Eddie Hausner/The New York Times/Redux

CLAUDE SITTON

A crusty old-school journalist with his sleeves rolled up and a drink waiting at the end of the day, Claude Sitton earned the moniker "dean of the civil rights beat" for his attention to detail, standards of excellence and capacity to land on his feet in almost any venue with the men, equipment and sources to write a comprehensive story on deadline.

To cover the Ole Miss story, Sitton, chief Southern correspondent for *The New York Times*, had six reporters and five white rental cars identical to those driven by the FBI and an airplane on standby to cover events as they moved between Oxford and Jackson, the state capital.

Karl Fleming, who shared the cost of the airplane with Sitton, described his associate as "a model for all civil rights reporters that

I knew anything about, an absolute model of quiet decorum and recti-tude and objectivity and I think... he remains in our heads the symbol and the icon of all the work that we did."[98]

And so it was in Mississippi, as Sitton and Fleming traversed the state on a plane the size of a small Cessna. *The New York Times* had the money to finance the equipment and Sitton had the sources to set up shop on short notice. That talent was crucial in Oxford as hotel rooms were scarce with more than 300 reporters and a large contingent of federal government officials needing housing. Sitton opted for the Ole Miss Motel, a string of rooms on University Avenue, a half-mile from campus, which he believed was connected to the Klu Klux Klan. Sitton recalled, "(It) was run by a fellow whose last name was Nail. We called him Rusty. We stayed there because we had been told that Rusty was a standing member of the Ku Klux Klan. We figured, if some of the thugs decided to burn down motels in Oxford, that it would not be Rusty Nail's place and quite a few reporters did the same thing. It was tense but very, very interesting."[99]

Not able to secure enough rooms for the whole *Times* delegation, one of the paper's reporters, McCandlish Phillips, a tall skinny guy, wound up sleeping in Sitton's clothes closet. Sitton stacked his papers neatly, kept his belongings in a travel-weary aluminum suitcase and tolerated the crowded conditions.

Sitton also installed a long-distance telephone trunk line in his motel room, giving him immediate access to long-distance lines needed to provide updates to his editors and to stay abreast of events. Accurate news was hard to come by that weekend. For Sitton, the owner of the Mansion restaurant turned out to be one of his best local sources.[100]

The Mansion, William Faulkner's favorite, was located in an old house off the nearby downtown Square. It served hot meals three times a day and was a center of community activity. When *Times* reporter Thomas Buckley violated local social norms Saturday by interviewing black residents accompanied by a female Ole Miss student, the owner of the Mansion called Sitton to warn him that Buckley's conduct was unacceptable. Fleming recalled that it was the only time he saw Sitton "lose his cool"—angrily letting Buckley know that his behavior was inappropriate and could be harmful to the newspaper's reputation.[101]

As the tension intensified and the action moved from Oxford to Jackson, Sitton assigned stories, often writing the lead story, while other reporters wrote the secondary stories. On Sunday afternoon, just as he finished dictating a report about the latest strategy calling for Meredith to enroll 10 a.m. Monday, Sitton learned Meredith was on campus. An anonymous source called with the news, but Sitton recognized the man's voice as that of Edwin O. Guthman, press secretary to Robert Kennedy. "I was taking in information on one telephone, and [on the other] I was dictating what's called a lead, a new lead, at the top of the story, to The New York Times... for the first edition. So, you know the pressures were pretty stiff."[102]

Sitton immediately hung up and called his best campus source, James Silver, an Ole Miss history professor whose liberal views would later get him run out of the state.

> Jim Silver's wife and his son were right there when they brought Meredith onto the campus, and they fed me the details. I already knew from Ed Guthman that he's definitely here. And so I got the details on what was going on the campus... I'd opened the line to New York on my spare phone and told New York that I was going to have to give them what we call a lead to a completely new story.
>
> I had the other phone to Jim Silver's house to his wife and his son. They were giving me information on one phone and I was dictating my story over the telephone, the new story, on the other telephone.[103]
>
> We did not have cell phones in that day. You know you couldn't go back to the motel room and plug a computer into a telephone line and transmit it over the line. I dictated to a dictating room at The New York Times that had six trained people taking dictation, and news would get through their typewriters very fast. They used stencils, they'd cut stencils, sometimes a paragraph at a time, and then copy boys would snatch the stencils out of their typewriters, rush to a machine, and grab 20 copies of the story,

which were circulated among the various editors, and that's the way that operated. And it worked pretty well. You had to learn how to dictate.[104]

After dark, the violence escalated, and the protestors turned on the reporters. A television truck was burned. Efforts were made to overturn cars driven by reporters. Equipment was pulled from cameramen's shoulders and smashed. Sitton explained:

> The people who were opposed to Meredith. They preferred to be isolated... As far as the rioters were concerned, many of them were actually thugs, just thugs. Some of them were students from Mississippi State who came up there, and I am not sure that any outsider would not have been a target there that night.
>
> I don't care whether they knew what was right or wrong, all the people, including the blacks, were under great pressure from the change that was going to revolutionize Mississippi, the culture, the social interactions, the economic picture and the politics. The mores' and values were going to be changed. I don't care whether you are black, white or whatever. The pressure was very great, and the people don't like change.[105]

The university public relations office issued press passes. As the viciousness escalated, the reporters tore the passes from their

Ole Miss student demonstrators.
Photo by Ed Meek.

Interviewing students on September 30.
Photo by Ed Meek

lanyards and ditched ties and coats. Some of the younger newsmen adopted the jeans and T-shirts of college students. Sitton's strategy for covering a demonstration was simple: "If it got rough, take off your coat, take off your shirt. Stomp on it in the dirt, put it back on and leave the last few buttons unbuttoned. Get it good and dirty."[106]

Sitton later went to campus to gather more material for his stories. Fear for his own safety never occurred to him. "You had to be there, you had to see it because, if you didn't, then you had to rely on what others told you, by members of the movement, or by officials. And you [knew] they shaped what they were telling you to their own interest."[107]

With four *New York Times* editions needing updates, he was "just too damn busy" to be afraid the night of September 30. "I got trapped the night of the riot. On the second trip up to the administration building, I got caught after I left between the marshals and the mob and for five minutes or so I scrambled under a car. The crowd was throwing rocks and everything at the marshals. I had a job to do with *The New York Times*... When you are working sixteen hours a day, sometimes you don't have that much time to be afraid. That is the truth."[108]

One of the white rental cars was destroyed by the rioters: "They got one of our Avis cars. [Fred] Powledge [of *The Atlanta Journal*] was driving it and I never forgave him for it. They broke out the windshield," Sitton recalled. "Of course, he could not help it. He drove it away from the riot scene with the broken windshield and parked it. Avis came and got it."[109]

Sitton's long tenure on the race beat set him apart from the other reporters and earned him the moniker "dean of the civil rights press corps." "I had the greatest newspaper job in the world. I had the opportunity to go out and find out the top story in the field, and get into the middle of it," Sitton explained." I wanted to tell what was going on, but more importantly, why."[110] To aid him he ditched the traditional stenographer's notebook for a smaller-half size version a stationer made for him in Atlanta. The smaller size fit neatly inside a coat pocket, making his identity as a reporter less obvious. It is now the standard notebook for journalists.

As the civil rights movement gained steam and created demands for more national coverage, organizations such as the NAACP begged for coverage, recognizing that, without the northern media covering their events, little interest could be generated outside the region. *The Times* frequently led the coverage, setting the agenda that other Northern newspapers followed. But the newspaper did not seek to impose its editorial views on its correspondents, directly them to report only what they saw or learned from viable sources.

"I knew the rules, and I tried to stick by them. I was not a member of the movement. I was, let's say, an observer, you know, a very interested observer, but I was not a member of the movement. I never presented myself as such," Sitton said.[111]

Sitton began as copy editor at *The New York Times* after writing for a wire service for six years. It wasn't long before he was reporting on civil rights. Management wanted a Southerner on the beat and sent Sitton south on a trial basis. He later recalled the advice of John Popham, the first Southern correspondent for *The Times*: "The facts of Southern life were rarely what they seemed to be, and almost never what the spokesman for an agitated constituency said they were."[112] Being a Southerner gave Sitton "a certain protective coloration" that enabled him to do the job better than perhaps someone else might have.[113] The Georgia native had a soft Southern drawl and the manners of a Southern gentleman under a tough-as-nails exterior.

He began covering the South in 1958 shortly after the first sit-ins in Greensboro, N.C., following every major development from then on, including Little Rock and the Freedom Rides. He earned his battle scars while serving on a Navy ship during World War II in the Pacific between 1943 and 1946.

Yet his heroes were not his wartime comrades, but E.W. Steptoe, an African-American farmer from Amite County, Mississippi, who called out local segregationists after they murdered a civil rights supporter named Howard Lee. Steptoe, the only registered black in a county with 3,500 blacks of voting age, served as president of the local chapter of the NAACP. The Student Non-violent Coordinating Committee (SNCC) had launched a voter registration drive that riled the residents of Liberty, Mississippi. Steptoe lived across the street from the white man, a state legislator and a childhood playmate, who murdered Lee. Steptoe, who was active in the voter registration drive, responded to news of the murder, telling reporters: "Glad to see y'all. I know I've got five minutes more to live, longs as you here."

"That's the kind of guy I respect. More courage than anyone I know," Sitton said.[114]

Sitton's journey to journalism began in the red clay of Conyers, Georgia, 25 miles from Atlanta. His father worked as a train conductor until he broke his back uncoupling a carload of skins destined for a shoe factory. Claude Sr. hailed from northwestern South Carolina. He bought a farm with his railroad settlement. Sitton's mother Pauline Fox, a teacher, was the daughter of a Methodist circuit minister in northern Georgia.

His parents taught him to treat blacks as individuals and with basic fairness. Growing up, he played with blacks and, as a teenager working in a grocery store, waited on them as customers.

"We were an atypical family. The litmus test in those days was whether you were pro or anti Talmadge... [Gov.] Gene Talmadge. We were anti. We didn't think he was respectable. Didn't like his racial views," Sitton said. "That was the South that taxed the right to vote and punished blacks for even trying. That was the South of poverty and peonage. The South of Jim Crow and lynch law. If you were black, you drank from a public water fountain marked 'colored.' You sat at the back of the bus and never at the white lunch counter. You bought what clothes you could afford without having the right to first try them on. And if you resisted, these and other indignities, repressions, and injustices, a white policeman would come and lock you up."[115]

A childhood incident profoundly affected Sitton's views of blacks as fellow citizens: "There was a very strong athletic type black fellow at the warehouse. Used to brag about his sexual prowess. One time, the whites grabbed him, tied a string around his penis and suspended him from the cotton scales so that he had to stand on his tiptoes. Didn't hurt him or injure his penis...[but] segregation was sort of a way of life that you didn't think about... you knew some things were wrong."[116]

When Sitton served in the Navy, he became accustomed to living alongside black crew members. His first experience was on a ship heading downstream on the Ohio River from Jeffersonville, Indiana. "There was a black cook and a couple of black stewards. There was one commode for the blacks and only three for 20 or 30 whites. Well the whites put up with that for one day; then the signs came down and we all used the same facilities," he recalled. "Well, you know, it's a little crowded on ship and that didn't bother anyone."[117]

After leaving the Navy in 1946, Sitton earned his journalism degree at Emory University. He worked for International News Service in 1949 and 1950 and for United Press International from 1950 to 1955 before heading to Ghana, which gained its independence in 1957, the first nation south of the Sahara to do so. Sitton worked as a press attaché at the U.S. Embassy. "There was [in Ghana] the end of colonialism still driven to some extent by the end of World War II, and there was some principle of self-determination," he said.[118] The

42

experience affected his world view, and he recognized a similarity between the Ghana citizens and their quest for civil rights and that of black Americans.

When Sitton first met Meredith in 1961 they talked about "the white-black-rich-poor issue" in Mississippi. Meredith called it "the most important learning experience of my lifetime," adding that it "influenced his relationship with the press," because Sitton never reported the conversation but used it to gain an understanding of Meredith's quest. The interview was arranged by NAACP Field Secretary Medger Evers. [119]

NEGRO AT MISSISSIPPI U. AS BARNETT YIELDS; 3 DEAD IN CAMPUS RIOT, 6 MARSHALS SHOT; GUARDSMEN MOVE IN; KENNEDY MAKES PLEA

Tear gas is used.
Mob attacks officers
2500 troops are sent to Oxford

By Claude Sitton

Oxford, Miss., Monday, October 1, James H Meredith, a 29-year-old Negro, was admitted last night to the University of Mississippi campus and was scheduled to enroll today in the all-white institution.

A riot broke out shortly after his arrival, and marauding bands of students and adults, many of whom were from other states, were still ranging through the campus and the town early today.

At least three [sic] men were killed, one of them unidentified. Fifty persons were being treated for various injuries in the University infirmary. Six United States marshals were shot, one was critically wounded.

Although the riot started at about 7:30 PM, Central Standard Time, Army troops did not arrive until 5 1/2 hours later.

43

About 200 military policemen arrived from Memphis shortly after 1 AM.

Army headquarters received word early today that about 200 more persons had joined the rioting mob and that the situation on the campus was very bad, the Associated Press reported. About 2500 regular Army military policeman and infantrymen were converging on Oxford. Army observers in Mississippi reported to headquarters that automatic weapons fire was being aimed at the registration building.

A small detachment of Mississippi National Guardsmen went to the aid of a besieged force of 300 deputy marshals in the university administration building. The marshals were under the command of top justice department officials, including Nicholas de B. Katzenbach, deputy attorney general.

For a time, it appeared that the marshals would not be able to hold the building, which is called the Lyceum. But barrage after barrage of teargas discouraged the writers, and they began to break up.

A number of other Mississippi National Guardsmen had arrived early today at the Armory on the eastern outskirts of town. But there was considerable delay before they began a drive to the campus.

Automobiles loaded with roughly dressed whites, some of whom were from Alabama, began pulling into the campus shortly after the state highway patrol withdrew from the campus entrances early last night.

Clouds of teargas billowed around the administration building.

The tree-dotted mall in front of the building had the appearance of a battlefield as students and adults massed behind Confederate battle flags and charged repeatedly toward the marshals.

Travel to and from the campus was extremely dangerous. Roving bands of students halted cars and questioned their occupants to determine if they were friend or foe.

At one point, a second mob began forming at Baxter Hall, a dormitory where Mr. Meredith reportedly was housed. Word passed through the mob at the administration building that an attempt to burn the dormitory would be made. But it did not materialize.

The troops were bombarded with bricks and sticks,

and obscenities were shouted at the men.

Five minutes later students brought a bulldozer up from a construction site. A yell went up from a nucleus of about 200 students among a milling throng of more than 1,000. Students and others moved in behind the bulldozer, which aimed straight for the main door of the administration building.

The plan seemed to be to abandon the machine at full throttle and let it plow wildly into the troops. But the 'dozer stalled and was quickly swallowed up in the clouds of tear gas.

Later, however, the students and their adult reinforcements retrieved the bulldozer and sent it crashing against the steps at the entrance of the building.

Others in the mob stole a fire truck and drove it around and around through the trees. At one point its driver sent it careening down the drive in front of the building, drawing a barrage of tear gas grenades.

Aside from the marshals, the chief targets of the rioters were newsmen. One of the dead was Paul Guihard, who carried press cards identifying him as a correspondent for Agence French Presse and the Daily Sketch of London.

The other man killed was Rae Gunter, 23 years old, of Abbeville, Miss., a small town north of here.

A spokesman at Oxford hospital said Mr. Gunter had died of a gunshot wound in the forehead. The cause of Mr. Guihard's death was not determined definitely.

William Crider, an Associated Press reporter from Memphis, was wounded slightly by birdshot. A number of other newsmen were beaten.

State highway patrolmen, who had made a halfhearted attempt to hold the students back, climbed into their prowl cars and left the campus at 9:10 PM.

Three students were taken prisoner in one clash with the deputy marshals. The federal men, although carrying side arms, depended chiefly on barrage after barrage of teargas to hold back their assailants.

One newsman said a man wearing a policeman's uniform was throwing bottles and rocks at the marshals.

One of the mob's charges on the Lyceum, the administration building, followed a harangue by former Maj. Gen. Edwin A.

45

Walker from the pedestal of a Confederate monument across the mall from the Greek-revival structure of white columns and brick masonry.

"Protest! Protest! Keep it up!" Mr. Walker shouted.

He did not advocate violence. But he told the students that help was coming from out of the state. He accused Mississippi officials of a "sellout" and named T.B. Birdsong, Commissioner of Public Safety.

The Rev. Duncan M. Gray, rector of St. Peter's Protestant Episcopal Church, stepped up on the pedestal and called on the students to end the violence. Some grabbed him and roughed him up.

He was led through the mob by an unidentified law-enforcement officer.

Mr. Walker then told the students he would give them his "moral support." He turned and strode up a walkway toward the Lyceum with 100 students following behind.

"Sic 'em, John Birch!" a student shouted from across the street.

The former general and his followers were greeted with a volley of teargas after some among them had begun throwing rocks and bottles at the marshals.

The riot indicated that if Mr. Meredith went ahead with plans to enroll as a student, his future would be hazardous. He is scheduled for registration this morning, under an agreement between Attorney General Robert F. Kennedy and Gov. Ross R. Barnett.

State troopers, university officials and the campus police made no attempt to break up the mob, which began massing at the Lyceum even before Mr. Meredith's arrival.

The 300 or more deputy marshals who ringed the building fired a barrage of teargas to force the mob back as it surged toward them.

A flaming missile was hurled atop a big Army truck used to transport the marshals. Its canvas cover began to burn.

A soldier climbed up and put the fire out. Members of the mob aimed squirts from a fire extinguisher at him.

The students then turned on the station wagon, which was loaded with equipment. They smashed its windows, ripped off its license plate and kicked dents in its sides.

Students let air out of the tires of three Army trucks

parked in front of the Lyceum building and tossed lighted matches at them.

Several state troopers looked on and laughed. Others walked away as the students charged in toward the deputy marshals, who were forced to fire the tear gas to protect themselves.

Governor Barnett's retreat followed the action of the United States Court of Appeals for the Fifth Circuit in finding him guilty of contempt for his defiance of orders to desegregate the university. He had been given until tomorrow to purge himself or face a $10,000-a-day fine and likely imprisonment.

Mr. Meredith was flown here yesterday in a two-engine border patrol plane from the United States Naval Air Station near Memphis. Besides the pilot, he was accompanied by John Doar, first assistant in the Justice Department Civil Rights Division, and another Federal official who was unidentified.

They were met at the University-Oxford airport on the outskirts of Oxford by Nicholas de B. Katzenbach, deputy attorney general, and Edwin O. Guthman, the Justice Department's public information chief.

Mr. Meredith climbed into a green Plymouth sedan with New York license plates. The car moved into a convoy of other automobiles and army trucks.

Mr. Meredith, wearing a gray suit, white shirt and dark tie, appeared calm. He carried a small, tan attaché case and a newspaper.

The deputy marshals arrived here by plane in two groups yesterday. There were 165 in the first contingent and 140 in the second.

The federal officials wore white helmet liners. Some wore riot vests bristling with tear gas canisters and cartridges. All carried riot clubs.

Students gathered in "The Grove," a tree shaded grassy mall in front of the Lyceum building, a neo-Greek revival building, as the marshals arrived.

They began to heckle the marshals. Some jeered and shouted such taunts as "nigger lover" and "we don't want Bobby Kennedy."

A campus source said the university's chancellor, John Davis Williams, had warned students against hooliganism. He told them there was agreement between the marshals and the highway patrolmen and said that any who interfered would incur the wrath of both groups.

As the marshals rolled onto the campus in the big Army trucks, Walker opened a news conference in the parking lot of the Ole Miss Motel.

He said he had been in touch with state and local officials. He said a "quite spontaneous" movement of thousands of men sympathetic to Governor Barnett's stand were heading for Oxford from all over the nation.

Some of the 2,200 Mississippi National Guard men ordered here after President Kennedy had placed them in federal service began reporting this morning at the Armory on Route Six East.

KARL FLEMING

Newsweek writer Karl Fleming, who grew up in a Methodist orphanage in North Carolina, brought to his reporting a disdain for violence and bullying he learned while wearing short pants. From this abhorrence of the misuse of power grew the critical eye of a reporter.

"I think my experience in the entirety of this thing [the race beat], I was so angry and so ashamed, that I was really probably too dumb to be afraid, and that was the thing. I was just angry all the time, and ashamed, and many nights," he recalled. "I would go back to my motel room and literally throw up. It was just so shameful, the thing, I mean, I saw white people do things to black people that were just almost incomprehensible."[120]

Fleming, a hard-working, hard-drinking, intense reporter, started his newspaper career in Wilson, North Carolina, after time in the U.S.

Navy and with two years of college. Before he was hired by *Newsweek* in 1961 and began reporting on civil rights, he worked for *The Atlanta Constitution*: "I could see right away that the civil rights story was going to be an epic and long-running one and I wanted to be in on it as long as possible."[121] And, he did, from the first major demonstration in Albany, Georgia, in 1961 through the 1965 Watts riots, where he was savagely beaten and left for dead.

Writing for *Newsweek* was different than writing for a newspaper. Stories did not bear bylines, as they were the result of multiple contributors. A solo editor polished the prose into crisp language using rich detail and in-depth interviews. The stories had a strong narrative thread that included detailed scene-setting, strong personalities and clarity of purpose. Stories on civil rights issues included more than basic facts. They blossomed with the refrains of music sung at demonstrations and the emotional pitch of the participants. The significance of the story was not left to the reader to ponder. As far as Fleming was concerned, there were no two sides to the civil rights story:

> Black people were treated terribly. They simply didn't have rights. That was an objective fact. There are no two sides to an issue. It was simply wrong. I'm not suggesting... that we weren't fair. We were scrupulously fair, had to be. God knows if you were caught doing something unfactual, it would have been the end of it all for you. So you had to maintain scrupulous integrity in the factual report, and I'm talking about what was going on in my heart, in my gut... The reporting was fair. I'm not saying that the weight of the facts didn't come down that made the Southern white institution look as if it had fallen down on the job, which it had. That was just a fact. We knew the moral weight was on the other side of the fence. So there was an intense, scrupulous effort to make absolutely sure that the so-called other side got its due day in court.[122]

In *Newsweek*'s six-and-a-half-page story about the crisis the magazine took its headline from William Faulkner's novel, *The Sound and the Fury*, which dealt with the how individuals experience change in social and cultural contexts, recognizing at the same time that the South harbors

Student demonstrators the night of September 30.
Photo by Ed Meek.

many cultures.[123] Faulkner, who was awarded both the Nobel Prize and the Pulitzer Prize for literature, haunted and inspired the people of Oxford and, by extension, Mississippi. Faulkner, significantly, appeared to accept the inevitability of integration, believing: "the white man had better take charge of it [*integration*] and control it, rather than have it thrust on him."[124]

Fleming's account of the riot pulled no punches, skewering state and federal leaders and detailing how a campus known for its beauty came to resemble a wasteland of burned out vehicles and empty tear gas containers. A second story in the "Press" section of the magazine provided a detailed story about Paul Guihard's murder. For Fleming: "It was the first assignment I've ever had where I was actually afraid for my life. It hurt to realize these were people from your own culture doing this."[125]

Safety was always a personal consideration, but it did not prevent Fleming from wading into the middle of a situation. Looking back, he found Ole Miss to be the most complicated, dangerous venue he covered on the race beat: "No place represented (more) the romanticized, glorious white history of Mississippi, its misty-eyed nostalgia and defiant pride."[126]

> The first time I saw James Meredith, I thought this man's got to be crazy. In the previous two years, there had been two black people who tried to get into it (Ole Miss and Mississippi Southern). They immediately slapped one in the insane asylum. The first guy they thought, any guy to try this must be crazy. The second guy, they framed him for stealing nine sacks of chicken feed. And put him in the penitentiary for nine years.
>
> So here was Meredith, five feet, six inches tall, 135 pounds, long eyelashes, delicate little face, tiny little voice, and I thought this guy's got to be nuts.[127]

Fleming teamed up with Claude Sitton of *The New York Times* at many civil rights venues, often sharing cars, meals and information while wading into tense situations. In Oxford, he also shared the rental costs of a small Cessna. Since *Newsweek* was a weekly publication, the men were not direct competitors, and the camaraderie was good for both of them. They often shared dinner and a drink after witnessing violence and controversy during long days on the road. Sitton more often than not picked the motel, relying on his deep sources and in 1962, other reporters on the civil rights beat often followed his lead in choosing lodging.

Fleming's room at the one-story brick Ole Miss Motel was just a few doors down from the rooms occupied by *The New York Times* and about a half-mile from campus. Sitton figured Klan ownership provided some safety from the possibility of fires, bombings and shotguns fired through the windows, not to mention accessibility to alcohol.[128]

> We were all working just on blind instinct. I think at that time in space we all must have had some kind of sense of vulnerability. I know I did," Fleming said. "I think we had a sense that somehow we weren't involved. It was the—it was the blacks and the whites, and we weren't either. We were some kind of third breed.[129]

On September 30, Fleming ate a hearty breakfast of country ham, eggs, grits and biscuits with Sitton at the Mansion Restaurant, seated in the booth favored by Faulkner, who had died a few months earlier.

Wandering down University Avenue toward the Illinois Central Railroad bridge that marked the main entrance to campus, the pair noted numerous out-of-state license plates on cars and pickup trucks. "The resistance fighters arriving were rough-looking, Snopesian charac-

Photo by Ed Meek

ters, many with angry faces and sagging bellies in a variety of working clothes," Fleming observed, linking the troublemakers to the rapacious characters in Faulkner's novels.[130]

Accompanied by *Newsweek* writer Peter Goldman and photographer Dan McCoy of Black Star Inc., Fleming arrived on campus around 8:10 p.m. shortly after President Kennedy's televised speech extolling the apparently successful arrival of Meredith. In fact, the battle was raging on campus as the president spoke. The men parked their car in the Circle, near the Lyceum. Academic buildings surround the greenspace, some dating from the early days of the university's founding more than a century before. The Lyceum is on the western side, the main entrance the eastern.

As Fleming walked through the greenspace he saw a battle in progress. Lone troublemakers and those in small groups of four or five men moved forward shouting obscenities while throwing bricks, wood and other construction material taken from a nearby building site. When the rioters came too close the marshals responded by lobbing tear gas sizzling over their heads, sending fumes across the acreage. The movement from the east was irregular, there was no clear leader, rather the pulsating crowd of angry white men seemed to feed off its collective anger. Their rage was focused on causing as much harm and danger to the university's symbolic citadel of learning as they could. And so it went throughout the night.

On the advice of Mississippi National Guardsmen, the trio headed to the Chemistry Building, south of the administration building. The billowing tear gas did little to move the mob away from the Lyceum because a westerly wind forced the fumes back toward it. Other reporters in the Chemistry building included WMPS radio reporters Harvey Tate and Don Stevens from Memphis, who watched their new Ford Falcon station wagon loaded with gear go up in flames.[131]

From his vantage point, Fleming watched the mob increase in number and age. Screaming rebel chants and throwing Molotov cocktails, the troublemakers continued their assault on the marshals, who stood stoically in line around the two-story building with its graceful Ionic columns. Around 9 p.m., a state police departed the campus in a line of some 68 cars, leaving the campus entrances unguarded, contending they were not equipped for battle. Fleming also noted that the mob had pulled back after the first gas canisters were lobbed. "They were congregated in one place and, if the police simply closed in on them they could—wouldn't have had any substantial difficulty simply herding them off the campus at that time."[132]

At this point, it appeared to Fleming that a detente was possible. The marshals called out "truce," and some of the rioters paused in their assault. But it was short-lived. According to Fleming, someone in the rear threw a brick and more bricks followed. Voices shouted, "We need General Walker. Give 'em hell, you rebels. Let's go gettum, boys."[133] Edwin Walker, a disgraced former U.S. Army general, stood by the Confederate statue, encouraging the protesters. He was later arrested and charged with insurrection.

The crowd in front of the Lyceum swelled as more rioters poured in with a variety of weapons, including high-powered rifles and shotguns. To Fleming, "The riot seemed to develop the energy of a cyclone, sweeping up everybody in its path and turning them into maddened animals. I had seen some bad things up to then in my native South, but nothing approaching this."[134]

Over the next two hours, the rioters acquired a fire truck, a bulldozer and cars, with the apparent intent of using them to break the marshal's line before smashing the front doors of the Lyceum. The goal was to grab Meredith and remove him from campus—dead or alive. The vehicles were stopped. Officials dragged the drivers out of the cabs, or, in the case of a driveless vehicle, they removed a brick wedged on the accelerator.

Fleming believed that, at this point, the Mississippi state troopers could have quelled the riot. Most of the rioters were huddled in the far corner of the Circle, and an efficient sweep would have pushed the attackers out of the area. Instead, the absence of the state police appeared to embolden the rioters.

Fleming observed about a dozen people with handkerchiefs over their faces entering the building. He heard breaking glass in nearby laboratories. The men appeared to be passing Molotov cocktails to men posted outside.

Fleming slipped out a side door and fled to the Lyceum. He borrowed a gas mask and went outside again. As he stood on the building's columned portico, bullets whizzed past his head and lodged in the doorframe at about eye level, missing him by three feet.

Fleming wrote later that he left Oxford filled with anger, not so much at what he called the rabble, i.e., "the ignorant and maddened white mob," but at Mississippi's elite, which included the politicians, Citizens Council and media. "They had, either by their active encouragement, as in the case of the governor and the Citizens Council, or by their silent abdication of responsibility, actually licensed and encouraged the rioters. They had done their state a great disservice, and Mississippi would pay that price and carry the stigma for years to come."[135]

> The main personal, emotional message that I came out of all of this with, and will carry with me forever, is the fact that even here, and I was thinking about this morning walking across this campus, even through that terrible, terrible night thousands of people were rioting, the Mississippi highway patrol, 68 cars strong leaving this campus in rows, departing the scene, not

upholding the law, the magnificent bottom line is that the entire force of the United States government, the United States Army was stationed on the campus of the University of Mississippi for the first time since the civil war. Two people got killed, dozens were injured, property damage, thousands, all to protect the constitutional right of one tiny black five-foot-nine American citizen. And that, I think is really the ultimate message that ought to come of this for everybody, for our country, because that's really what this country stands for.[136]

Richard Valeriani of NBC said Fleming "used to get some good quotes because he'd dress up in his shit-kicker shoes and his good ole boy khakis and the hat with the toothpick in his mouth. He'd sidle up to these boys and talk to them. His drawl got a lot stronger in those days."[137] Other times, with his hair cut short and wearing tailored shirts, ties and dark suits, he often passed for a federal agent, another disguise that enabled Fleming to get close to the story.

Fleming also admits that he was brazen, arrogant, confrontational and occasionally reckless on the civil rights beat. He drank Jack Daniel's and smoked unfiltered Camels:

But I was never so arrogant as to think that anything that I did was anything on the par with the great black people who were putting their lives on the line every day. I don't know a single reporter who covered that era who had in any thought that "this story is going to make me a celebrity." I think reporters of this era—God knows, it's beginning to sound sure enough like an old fart talking—we were members of the working class and proud to be so. I don't know anybody who did it for the money. God knows the pay in my first job paid 30 bucks a week. In fact, all the reporters I knew had a kind of contempt for money and people whose main goal in life was to make it. Like publishers, right. I was in awe of black people who laid their lives on the line. We got to leave, not often, but we did get to pack our bags and go home to Atlanta or wherever we lived. They had to stay there, and often they lost their lives.[138]

KILL THE REPORTERS!

Contributors Karl Fleming and others

Newsweek, October 15, 1962

When newsmen checked in at the University of Mississippi to cover the growing integration crisis two weeks ago, two waggish photographers offered unofficial "Citation for Bravery" cards that read: "The above War Correspondent served with honor in the Reb-Fed battles at Oxford, Ole Miss..." Intended as humor, this citation turned out early last week to be a bitter, grisly joke.

For on Sunday night newsmen were beaten and shot at and one was killed in the savage riot that swirled furiously around the graceful old Lyceum building on the Ole Miss campus. In dispatches that had the ring of battle report, correspondents told how a mob of 2,500 students and rednecks hunting trouble, laid siege to the Lyceum and turned the grove of trees in front of it, normally the haunt of handholding couples, into a battle field. Reports of the bloody riot commanded huge headlines from Moscow to Uganda, Tokyo to Johannesburg.

At first university officials had expected only some 50 newsmen to cover the historic enrollment of James Meredith. But as Gov. Ross Barnett's defiance of Federal court orders for Meredith's registration grew more intransigent, the story climaxed by the riots of Sunday night and Monday attracted an army of correspondents. More than 330 reporters, photographers, and radio and television newsmen descended on Oxford, some sleeping in their cars, others packed half-dozen to a room in a single motel and a hotel. There were the big names of journalism - Bob Considine, covering for the Hearst syndicate, and Bill Mauldin, drawing his Chicago Sun-Times cartoons on scene - as well as lesser names. Most worked round the clock (Western Union added six persons to its one-woman Oxford staff to handle a total of some 250,000 words of copy), with little time to relax over $5-a-pint bootleg bourbon (Mississippi is legally dry).

The day the riots erupted, Paul Guihard, 30, a red bearded, fun-loving reporter for Agence France Presse, flew from New York to the state capital at Jackson and attended a meeting of the segregationist White Citizens Council. He concluded, in a telephoned dispatch to New York, that "the Civil War never came to an end." It was his last dispatch. A few hours later, in the war at Ole Miss, Guihard was shot in the back. His body was found facedown in some bushes.

As is always the case with mobs, newsmen were prime targets for the barrage of bottles, Molotov cocktail, and bricks. Shouts of "Let's kill all the reporters!" rang out, but newsmen literally risked their lives to cover the mob's charges. Reporters fast learned to hide their official Ole Miss press credentials and even to shuck their suit jackets, the sure sign of the "outsider." The more cautious worked behind the camouflage of "Ross is Right" buttons.

For photographers, it was even worse. Cameras, capable of recording the faces of members of a mob, were dead giveaways. Telenews cameraman Gordon Yoder of Dallas and his wife were attacked in their car and hoodlums destroyed $3,000 worth of equipment. When Yoder appealed to a state highway patrolman for help, the policeman only grinned. "I've been through a lot of tough spots," said Yoder, who spent a year in Korea, "but this is the worst thing I have ever experienced."

AP Memphis reporter Bill Crider, running through the mob and choking on teargas, was flattened by shotgun fire. It was three hours before all the buckshot was removed from his back.

The rioting that night and the next day in the center of Oxford gave many reporters a rare opportunity for enterprising, even distinguished, reporting. The Denver Post's John Rogers, passing as a redneck, stalked former Maj. Gen. Edwin A. Walker, and next day told Post readers how Walker directed the mob's actions. The Detroit News' Tom Joyce telephoned a vivid account of "eight terrifying hours" under siege in the Lyceum, site of the Ole Miss press room...

Courtesy of Pamela Dorman

MICHAEL DORMAN

Newsday reporter Michael Dorman came to Oxford curious about what William Faulkner might have thought about Meredith. He saw parallels to the crisis in Faulkner's novel *Intruder in the Dust*, in which a white mob attacks the county jail intent on lynching an innocent black man.[139] Faulkner wrote the novel in 1948 to tackle the simmering racial discord of his native land writing later that "the premise being that the white people in the south, before the North or the Govt. or anybody else owe and must pay a responsibility to the negro."[140]

Relationships between the races peppered Faulkner's novels, as did the mixed ambiance of the South. He was more liberal than his neighbors but less moderate than activists would have liked. His sentiments, expressed in his novels, stories, essays and public appearances, appeared contradictory. While conceding that Mississippi was locked into a system of white privilege and black deprivation, his views often reflected the Southern conservative's belief that the South would mend its ways in its own time. Faulkner contended: "The watchword of our flexibility must be decency, quietness, courtesy, dignity; if violence and unreason come, it must not be from us."[141]

It was in this context that Dorman, a veteran reporter for *Newsday* known for his in-depth reporting and his personable, literate style, sought out a Faulkner family member for an opinion on the issues.

Upon arriving in Oxford, Dorman visited Faulkner's fresh grave in St. Peter's Cemetery. The gravestone had yet to be erected, yet a steady stream of visitors had created a path from the street.

Dorman then visited the town Square, which Faulkner described in *Intruder In the Dust* as dominated by the two-story white stucco courthouse and "amphitheatric lightless stores."[142] Shops, including a grocery store and hardware store, shared the sidewalks with attorneys' offices and Neilson's department store, which had opened its doors in 1839. Men in dungarees sprawled on benches outside the courthouse and passed the day. No bars or taverns existed, as Mississippi was still a dry state in 1962. Comparing the real with the fictional, Dorman observed that little had changed.

The Confederate statute, erected in 1907 with the help of William Faulkner's ancestors, stood in front of the courthouse, which was rebuilt after the Union army burned the original structure in 1864. The plaque at the base memorialized Confederate dead from Lafayette County who "gave their lives in a just and holy cause." Later, Dorman reflected, "This 'just and holy cause' remained alive in the minds and hearts of many Oxford residents on that sunny September afternoon in 1962. Perhaps, as much or more than most other Southerners,

Lafayette County Courthouse circa 1962

they were carrying on the bitter struggle to preserve what they considered 'the Southern way of life.'"[143]

To learn where the Faulkner family stood on the race question, Dorman approached William's younger brother, author John Faulkner, who was a mirror image of Faulkner. Both were short men with white hair and wispy mustaches.[144] The interview, filed before James Meredith arrived on campus, would later prove that Dorman had come to the right place.

At Faulkner's home, John's wife, Lucille, suspicious of northern reporters, asked Dorman if he were "friend or foe." In Oxford, this same question had been asked of "Yankees" since Reconstruction. Dorman's self-effacing charm convinced Lucille he was a "southerner at heart." As the New Yorker entered John's rambling two-story house filled with family antiques, redolent of the past and as Southern as bourbon, he felt as if he were "walking into one of William Faulkner's novels."[145]

John was no fence-straddler on the Ole Miss crisis. Gov. Barnett, he told Dorman, "speaks for us. He is supporting the Constitution of the state of Mississippi and the Constitution of the United States. We will do whatever he tells us to do."[146]

Mississippi lawyer Phil Stone, Faulkner's mentor and a model for William Faulkner's hero in *Intruder in the Dust*, had told *The Miami Herald* that he, too supported Barnett. He added: "I don't understand why the Negro can't be left the way he is, a kind and gentle and, most of all, a happy race. He is making progress on his own and pushing him the way the NAACP is only creates hatred and bitterness... I wouldn't care too much if Meredith came to Ole Miss if I thought he was the only Negro who would be enrolled. But next year it will be ten more. This is just the beginning and it must be stopped."[147]

Stone's perception, of course was highly accurate, even if the media missed the obvious. As historian Vincent Harding noted, the story in Oxford was not about one man, but about all men. "We have never wanted to be simply integrated into America as it exists... we want to participate in that transformative process, not simply to come in and sit down."[148] And, that, of course, is what the segregationists feared most.

John Faulkner (left) with his sons, Jimmy and Chooky, and John's wife Lucille.
Faulkner family photograph.

John Faulkner, meanwhile, echoed his brother's belief that the South should be allowed to work out its own integration. "This is actually a fight on whether the states have any rights left. The Supreme Court desegregation decision of 1954 is unconstitutional. It is based on social theory, not law."[149] He was confident Mississippi would solve its race problems on its own, at its own pace, predicting, "It's not going to come to violence. It's going to come to a courtroom fight."[150] The weekend would show that he was wrong on several counts.

By Friday, September 28, the federal courts had ruled that James Meredith was to be admitted to the university early the next week. And the civil rights standoff between Mississippi and the federal government, which Faulkner predicted in 1948, would soon have brother fighting brother in the battle over integration. In twenty-four hours, John Faulkner's two sons, Jimmy and Murry (Chooky) would be at each other's throats.

Like his great-great-grandfather, William C. Falkner, who had served as a colonel in the Confederate Army, Chooky spelled his surname without a "u." His older brother Jimmy used the "u" which William had added in 1919 upon the self-publication of *Marionettes*, his first book. Both brothers served in the military, Jimmy as a Marine fighter pilot in World War II, and Chooky as a captain on active duty in the Mississippi National Guard. Like their parents, the brothers held segregationist views. On September 30th, however, those attitudes and loyalties were tested on the university campus.

When President John F. Kennedy ordered the federalization of the Mississippi National Guard, Captain Murry C. Falkner put on his Army uniform and headed to the Oxford armory, a half-mile from his parents' home on University Avenue. Across the state, more than 11,000 men were called up, including the governor's son. Most never left their armories. Kennedy moved quickly to federalize the guard, fearing Barnett would activate the guard first, pitting the Mississippi units against the federal government.

Falkner, commander of the Oxford company unit attached to the 108th Armored Cavalry Regiment, assembled his 63 men and led them in the Oath of Allegiance. As citizen-soldiers they swore to "support and defend the Constitution and laws of the United States against all enemies, foreign and domestic . . ." At that moment Falkner was not a Southerner but an American soldier, pledged to honor his obligation to his country. Under orders from Assistant Attorney General Nicholas Katzenbach, Falkner headed to campus around 9 p.m., leading the first military units to provide assistance to the besieged marshals. He would end up with a broken arm and bullet holes in his Jeep before the Jeep even reached the Lyceum. His obligation was further tested a few hours later when Chooky found himself facing Jimmy driving a bulldozer toward the Lyceum.

William Faulkner's niece, Dean, first cousin to Jimmy and Chooky, wrote of their confrontation in her memoir, *Every Day By the Sun*:

> Jimmy Faulkner was one of the men who commandeered a bulldozer at a building site and drove it towards the Lyceum. Klansmen with shotguns and dynamite followed the bulldozer like

infantry behind a tank. Their plan was to storm the Lyceum, drag Meredith out, and kill him. Chooky's arm had been broken when a brick was thrown into his Jeep, but he was still in command, his arm in a sling fashioned out of an ammunition belt. Before Jimmy could get to the Lyceum, Chooky stood in the street blocking his path. Jimmy could not bring himself to run over his brother. Instead, he rammed the bulldozer into an oak tree, trying to bring it down so riflemen could use it for cover. The bulldozer's engine stopped; FBI agents swarmed the machine, and Jimmy ran. He was not caught. Later, Chooky was awarded the highest military decoration for service outside a theatre of war.[151]

Years after the riot, Chooky Falkner observed tongue in cheek, "It's hard to feel brotherly love toward someone who is trying to kill you."[152]

But before this collision of Fa(u)lkners, Dorman roamed the Square looking for cigarettes. He stopped at the Gathright-Reed drugstore where the owner, Mac Reed, once wrapped Faulkner's manuscripts for mailing. When informed federal marshals had entered the campus, Dorman raced to his rental car and backed out of his hotel parking space only to discover the car had a flat tire: "Of all the times for a flat, this was the worst."[153]

He caught a ride to the campus where he learned reporters were banned from entering. At a highway patrol checkpoint Dorman noticed that students were being waved through. He took off his tie, hid his notebook under his jacket, and strolled past the troopers. Making his way to the Lyceum, now surrounded by a line of U.S. marshals, he "watched the crowd build from a small group of good-natured students and faculty members" and gradually form a mob that attacked the marshals. Dorman was standing on the steps of the Lyceum when U.S. Chief

Bulldozer the morning after the riot.
Photo by Ed Meek.

Marshal James McShane gave the order to fire tear gas shortly before 8 p.m. The Lyceum corridors filled with wounded and bloody marshals where, along with other reporters, Dorman watched President Kennedy make his televised appeal:

> The eyes of the nation and all the world are upon the students of Ole Miss and upon all of us. And the honor of your university, and state, are in the balance. I am certain the great majority of the students will uphold that honor. You have a new opportunity to show that you are men of patriotism and integrity. For the most effective means of upholding the law is not the state policeman, or the marshals, or the National Guard. It is you.[154]

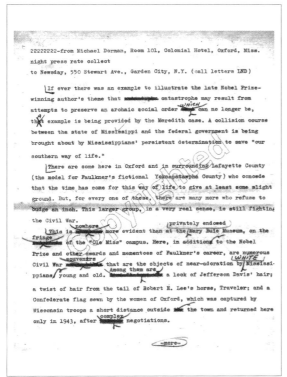

In the darkness the riot raged on. Dorman stayed up all night until reinforcements arrived. He witnessed the final scene as military police, joined by Mississippi National Guardsmen, fixed bayonets and drove the remaining rioters from the campus.

Dorman couldn't remember when he'd last eaten. At dawn, he returned to the Lyceum, phoned the *Newsday* office, and joined a chow line in the corridor. Except for a few chunks of bread and tomato juice, all the food was gone, he wrote:

Michael Dorman's telegram to Newsday,
courtesy University of Mississippi Archives

Tears still streamed from our eyes. We were sweaty, unkempt, unshaven. We had bummed cigarettes most of the night. The Coke and cigarette machines had long since run out of supplies. A package of Lifesavers in my pocket, coated with pipe tobacco that had dropped out of the pouch, had provided me and several of my companions with our only nourishment. We had not slept, and there was no indication that we would be getting any sleep soon. But we felt, for the first time all night, that we were safe. The United States Army was taking over now.[155]

OXFORD, 1962, FAULKNER NOVEL COME TRUE

Newsday, Oct. 1, 1962

By Michael Dorman

Oxford, Miss. - This hate scarred university town, where Negro James Meredith is trying to crumple a segregation barrier that has endured for 114 years, is the heart of William Faulkner country. And with each passing day the Meredith case is stacking up ever-increasing evidence to prove the truths woven in the literary fabric of Faulkner's work.

If ever there was an example to illustrate the late Nobel prize-winning author's theme that catastrophe may result from attempts to preserve an archaic social order which can no longer be, an example is being provided by the Meredith case. A collision course between the state of Mississippi and the federal government is being brought about by Mississippians' persistent determination to save "our southern way of life."

There are some here in Oxford and surrounding Lafayette County (the model for Faulkner's fictional Yoknapatawpha county) who concede that the time has come for this way of life to give at least some slight ground. But, for every one of these, there are many more who refuse to budge an inch. This larger group, in a very real sense, is still fighting the Civil War.

This is nowhere more evident than at the privately endowed Mary Buie Museum, on the fringe of the "Ole Miss" campus. Here, in addition to the Nobel Prize and other awards, and mementos of Faulkner's career, are numerous Civil War souvenirs that are the objects of near-adoration by white Mississippians young and old. Among them are a lock of Jefferson Davis's hair; a twist of hair from the tail of Robert E. Lee's horse, Traveler, and a Confederate flag sewn by the women of Oxford, which was captured by Wisconsin troops a short distance outside the town and returned here only in 1943, after complex negotiations.

A few houses down the street from the museum is the home of one of Oxford's most zealous crusaders for preserving the southern way of life. He is Faulkner's brother, John, also an author, whose works include Dollar Cotton, Men Working, and Chooky. At 61, with his white hair and wispy mustache, he is a carbon copy of William, who was four years his senior.

John Faulkner lives in a home that could have come straight out of one of his brother's novels. Built about 1830, it is a rambling two-story affair with huge, high ceilinged rooms and a turret-like effect in front. To get to it from the street, you must walk down a narrow foot path about 100 yards long, lined by towering oaks and evergreens grown so close together that they give the eerie effect they are closing in on you.

In his front parlor, filled with antiques, John Faulkner sits in a rocking chair and drags slowly on a cigaret as he explains his adamance in defending the southern way of life from what he considers encroachment by the federal government and Negroes such as Meredith. "We lived under Negro rule down here during the Reconstruction Period," he said. "They not only durn near starved the white people, but they starved themselves, too. They are just not the equal of the white people. The tragedy of this (Meredith case) is that the colored people get hurt by it. The white people aren't getting hurt."

Faulkner said he and a majority of Mississippians are solidly behind Gov. Ross Barnett's refusal to bow to federal court orders to enroll Meredith. "This is actually a fight on whether the states have any rights left or not," he said.

67

Faulkner said his brother had confided his position on desegregation to him before his death several months ago, but declined to discuss what the position was. William Faulkner, although he portrayed many of his fictional Negro characters sympathetically, stirred up a dispute a few years ago with a statement that was regarded by some as an attack on integration efforts and by others as merely a joke. The director of the Mary Buie Museum, Mrs. Herron Rowland, who grew up with the Faulkner boys, said: "I expect Bill would be on the fence over this Meredith business if he were still alive."

On the front steps of the "Ole Miss" Lyceum building, most students questioned in a random poll yesterday said they preferred to see the university closed than to attend classes with Meredith. Typical was the comment of a 19-year-old sophomore from Memphis: "I don't want to see 'Ole Miss' integrated. It would have social reverberations that would last 1,000 years. It would change the whole social structure of the South. There would probably be total social integration— mongrelization of the races. I don't want my grandchildren and great-grandchildren to be half nigger."

A 19-year-old blonde coed from Greenville summed up the minority view: "I would definitely rather see Meredith a student here than see the University close. I don't think there would be any violence if he were admitted, although he'd probably have to listen to some pretty nasty names tossed at him. I know this—I am a lot more interested in whether I can finish my education than in whether he is admitted."

A Methodist minister from nearby Bruce, Miss., visited the campus yesterday at the request of several members of his congregation who were concerned about their children here. "What bothers me," he said, "is that they were a lot more concerned about the possibility of the university being closed to their children than they were about the ethical implications of whether Meredith should be admitted."

DAN RATHER

Dan Rather was a fledgling network correspondent for CBS when he began covering the South as a Texan, a Westerner, not as a Southerner. For Rather, the events in Oxford were a seminal event in American history that also marked a change in how the news was covered and how the American public received its news.

In the post-World War II era, sales of televisions had risen rapidly because of the Baby Boomers' desire for home entertainment. Consumers, however, preferred newspapers and news magazines for information and commentary. TV news shows were a mere 15 minutes, and viewership of public affairs programs was just beginning. The young medium began earning its stripes with live coverage of the 1954 Senate hearings led by communist-hunter Sen. Joseph McCarthy. To grab the public's attention, the medium went looking for another big event.

Civil rights coverage became that event. Perhaps by choice, perhaps by opportunity, television exposed the ugly realities of the South to a nationwide audience. The stark and dramatic images portrayed through film were hard to ignore. According to Robert Northshield, an NBC producer, the civil rights movement offered an ideal platform for broadcast news to portray serious issues. Television's evening news with its para-social connection with the audience attracted an audience tired of waiting 24 hours to get the news in the next day's paper. The coverage of the Ole Miss riot the night of September 30 contributed to the change. The dramatic images of the riot flooded the airwaves the next day, bringing into living rooms the horror of damage, destruction and military units on a college campus. Or, as Rather noted:

> They could believe that people were set in their ways, and that moving from the Civil War and slavery period to the present was difficult. Once they saw it on television. Once they saw people actually shooting at U.S. marshals, officers of the law, including Mississippi state troopers, officers of the law, officers of the court, throwing things and trying to harm U.S. soldiers, this was a shock to the country's nervous system, and a shock to our national conscience. Once that happened, once that shock reverberated through the national consciousness, coverage of the civil rights movement increased steadily.[156]

The next year, network evening news was lengthened to 30 minutes. A Roper report concluded that television was the nation's primary source of news, by a slight margin, and had widened its lead as the "most believable" source of news while the nation's "most desired medium." That year, 1963, was also the year network news became available in all 48 contiguous states.[157]

Rather was in the vanguard of civil rights broadcasters. He started his career working part time at the *Houston Chronicle* and at KTRH radio, before making a name for himself at KHOU-TV in Houston. He landed at CBS in 1962 as chief of the Southwestern bureau based in Dallas. His assignment was to cover the civil rights movement. This he did with his combative personality, Texas drawl and the

Broadcast cameraman on the
steps of the Lyceum.
Photo by Ed Meek

determination to get the story no matter how difficult or challenging the situation. "The coverage of the movement... was never the same after what happened at Ole Miss in 1962. After that a lot of people who didn't pay attention, some who didn't want to pay attention paid attention, and most importantly political leaders."[158]

Ole Miss was the cutting edge of change in television news and a pivotal assignment for Rather. In 1962, he was home only 31 days as he criss-crossed the South covering one hot spot after another. Having attended segregated schools, he was familiar with the issues. A childhood bout of rheumatic fever had kept him bed-ridden for three years. He spent this time reading daily newspapers his father brought home, and listening to the radio, both of which gave him a view of the world outside Houston and an ear for narrative. His maternal grandmother was from Mississippi. The tales and traditions of the old Confederacy woven into his life-experience helped prepare him for reporting on James Meredith.

Texas, while segregated and a former member of the Confederacy, was as much or more Western than Southern, as in Deep South, which isn't to say was any better or any worse, but it was and it is different. It is unique. So is, as I learned, Mississippi; yes, Mississippi is closer in its ways and traditions perhaps to Alabama, Georgia, South Carolina than to Texas, but this is the point—Mississippi is different. It is unique.[159]

In the weeks leading up to September 30, Rather found the state's population dealing with Meredith's pending enrollment in a variety of ways, some of them intimidating. There were threats of bodily harm. High-ranking politicians and low-lifes alike attempted to coerce and pressure him. But they didn't stop him. He deflected the insults and frustrations because he understood Southern tradition and its importance as the South came to terms with the 20th Century. At the same time, he realized the events at Ole Miss had "changed the course of our country's future."[160]

According to Rather, Oxford "became a hell hole" during the riot that consumed the campus. It was, he said, comparable to the "ninth circle of Dante's hell . . .Tear gas, gunshots that first sounded like pistol shots, then maybe .22 rifle shots, then shotgun shots. Anybody who knows weapons knows a shotgun's close range, among the most dangerous weapons you can possibly have."[161]

The violence became personal to Rather when a man wielding a crowbar approached his crew intent on smashing their equipment. The man was turned away, Rather said, after witnesses blocked his path. "I'm not looking for sympathy," he said. "It's what we sign-up to do... The pictures out of Ole Miss in Oxford, the time of this insurrection... I use the word measurably, spoke for themselves. One didn't need much narration; you didn't need to write much to it."[162]

And whether it's a war zone far away or a war zone at home, and again make no mistake, for this short period, this became a war zone, which is to say people were firing real bullets; people had real intentions to kill other people on a fairly wide scale... The threats, the threats were constant; they were real, not imagined.[163]

Dan Rather at the Ole Miss airport.
Photo by Ed Meek.

Mississippi's political establishment viewed the media as a scourge; especially those who descended on the state from perceived "liberal Yankee" news organizations. CBS was frequently tagged as the "colored broadcasting company" and criticized for "sitting in New York City and judging the South" when the North had its own issues with race.

According to Rather, the press was there to do the job defined for them by the Founding Fathers and contained within the First Amendment:

> A reporter who's worthy of the name of professional journalist, the main part of the job, is to bear witness... Our job was to be as honest a broker of information as we could be, to do quality journalism, integrity... any journalist again worthy of the name must insist on being independent when necessary. And so it was during this time, to pull no punches, play no favorites and, to use the old line, to report without fear or favor.[164]

It was often a challenge for broadcasters to bear witness. A broadcast reporter was accompanied by a cameraman wielding a bulky film camera, another man operating lights and a third man for sound. Film was used, not video or digital equipment. Film had to be processed in a lab, which took time.

During the weeks and months Rather was in Mississippi, he learned that network allegiances were meaningless if a local station chose to be difficult. For example, at the network affiliate in Jackson, WLBT, some 160 miles to the south, the station manager agreed to feed Rather's news material to the network but reported later the film was "lost in the processor."

"I looked at him and we each knew what had happened," Rather recalled.[165]

In contrast, the owner of WREC-TV (now WREG-TV), 70 miles northwest in Memphis, whom Rather described as a caricature of a Southern colonel with a shot of bourbon in his hand and a Confederate pedigree, told Rather and his crew:

> I don't like what's going on, none of it. Matter of fact, I'm not too fond of you or your people. Nothing personal, understand. I

just don't like you. But I want you to know one thing. We may be country, but we care about what you're doing as much as you care about what you do. We're professionals. I'm sizing you up to see if you are. And if you are, you'll find out that whatever you need from us, you're going to get."[166]

The CBS crew passed muster. Rather and his crew worked out of the station located in the basement of the Peabody Hotel as needed, garnering the respect of their peers at the station and often relying on the skills of a hired driver who drove a fast Corvette.[167]

Housing was also an issue. Rather recalled a motel owner between Memphis and Oxford who put up a sign, hand-penciled on cardboard, proclaiming rooms were available, except: "No dogs, niggers or reporters allowed."[168] Rather, dressed impeccably to signal that he was a professional, walked into the office and confronted the motel owner. It was pure Rather—pugnacious and determined to make a point. His team did not spend the night there.

At the Ole Miss Motel in Oxford Rather had to deal with another important logistical issue. The switchboard closed at night making it impossible to receive calls from the network or anyone else. By September 30, however, the owner had hired an employee to work the switchboard overnight.

Rather and other journalists faced threats, which crossed socio-economic lines reaching into the highest level of Mississippi society: "The threats, the dangers were to life and limb. There were people, this is not imagined, this is not hyperbole, there were people who would sidle up to journalists, including this one and including the cameramen, soundmen and say in that under-voice, 'We know where you're staying,' and then slide away into the crowd... that kind of thing, of course, will really pierce your heart. It's one thing for them to say we know what motel you're staying in."[169]

The dangers also played a role in determining how the story would be covered.

According to Rather, when he arrived on campus the evening of September 30 with cameraman Wendell Hoffman, the first order of business was to determine where to position themselves to film

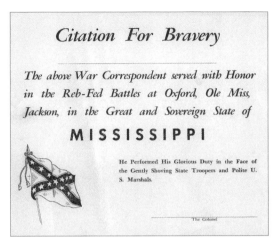

Courtesy of University of Mississippi Archives.

the action. The cumbersome cameras and sound equipment made it difficult to move around quickly. The choice was inside the Lyceum, the safer option and the headquarters of the unfolding drama, or outside in the crowd, where access to a telephone booth was more feasible. Recognizing that "the Tenth Commandment of journalism is that no story is worth a damn unless you can get it out,"[170] they opted for outside, spending most of the night in the Grove, a grassy 10 acres just inside the main gate and steps away from the Circle where the riot was underway.[171] It was there that Rather believes he briefly met Paul Guihard.

To avoid becoming targets, his team (in addition to Hoffman, he was working with Laurens Pierce and freelancer Dick Perez), Rather developed a four–pronged approach: turn on the battery-powered lights, film for 15 seconds, turn off the lights, and then run to another location to avoid being pelted by bricks and worse.[172] "But let's make no mistake about it that dangers to journalists were real. These were dangers to limb and to life... Many were hurt; many were wounded."[173] In addition to the murder of Guihard, a man from nearby Abbeville was killed and 160 marshals wounded. The Lyceum would become a temporary hospital, its basement and bathrooms sheltering the injured until medical care arrived.

Television rose to the occasion, bringing images of destruction and violence into the living rooms of viewers. The black-and-white images of burning cars, buildings bathed in tear gas and armed federal officials on a college campus turned heads. Ethical values played an important role. Rather noted: "My bosses in New York were rock-ribbed when it came to reporting the news without fear or favor to anyone, including their own affiliates."[174] Yet, he acknowledged that the danger of losing objectivity was there in the middle of the chaos. "Your guard had to be up. You had to protect your reporting from the biases of others—and yourself—and you knew it, because you knew this was a truly important story."[175]

I don't agree that this reporter was courageous during this time. There were courageous journalists. I'm sorry to inform you I was not among them. I was here. I did my best. I'm not above sort of inflating my role anywhere but courage is too—I like the word. I've used the word because I like to be associated with it. But I don't stand before you as someone to say I was courageous. I was here to do a job.[176]

THE PRESIDENT AND THE UNIVERSITY OF MISSISSIPPI

A Special CBS Report

Sept. 30, 1962

Segment reported by Dan Rather

The federal government's moves today in Oxford were swift and thorough. More than 300 helmeted U.S. marshals climaxed fast moving events of the afternoon when they poured out of twin-engine transport planes on the tiny Oxford landing strip. The marshals were armed with teargas guns and night-sticks. Chief United States Marshal McShane, who got pushed around Wednesday when he unsuccessfully tried to get Meredith on campus, personally directed the marshals' moves today. Whereas Wednesday, he had on a business suit, he also had on a helmet.

McShane quickly herded his men onto troop carriers which raced along roads surrounding the university campus, as awed spectators watched in silence. Mississippi lawmen hastily resumed their positions at the University gates, but they too were silent when the federal men and school registrar came on campus.

The federal government's pressure today started sixteen miles north of the campus when soldiers of the United States Army pitched camp. The camp was staged in an area where Union and Confederate troops are said to have bivouacked a century ago.

Moving across the state line from Memphis with army trucks and jeeps in the wee hours of the morning, today troops took to the weeds and erected a complete tent city in less than twelve hours. All traffic was stopped by armed soldiers and detoured around the campus.

Paratroop Major William Coach cautiously explains the purpose for the bivouac: "The unit setting up behind us is the 70th engineer Battalion from Fort Campbell, Kentucky. And we've been ordered in here to set up a tent city to be used by the federal marshals as required, and then to support the marshals logistically to the extent of housing them, feeding them, providing them with emergency medical treatment if required, and gasoline and oil for their vehicles."

"Now, are all of the soldiers and vehicles here members of an engineering unit?"

"No, not all of them are. There are about twenty-five of us who are paratroopers who have been detached as individuals."

"Major, speaking as an individual, how do you personally feel about such an assignment as this?"

"It's an assignment, and as a soldier I do as I'm told. I swore an oath to uphold and defend the Constitution, and this I will do to the best of my ability."

"You don't happen to know if there are any Mississippi boys in this contingent, do you?"

"No, we didn't stop to ask."

MOSES NEWSON

Baltimore Afro-American reporter Moses Newson was among the few black reporters assigned to cover the integration crisis, an assignment made even harder when law enforcement banned black reporters from campus. That did not deter him. "They tried to keep people from doing what they had a right to do, by using the warning that violence could occur," he fumed, still angry about the ban.[177]

A telegram sent by his city editor to the university had done little to change the situation. Pat Smith, director of the university news service, justified his position, saying: "We have a very small [campus] police force here. As you realize, the situation is tense. It is for your own protection. We felt like you should not be on campus."[178]

Mainstream newspapers seldom hired black reporters and few had viable black sources. Stories were written from a majority white view, or as Newson noted: "They were very often written from a point of view that was not from our point of view."[179] As such the African-American press provided a valuable and vital pipeline of information for blacks seeking information on stories of interest. Covering civil rights stories, however, came with personal challenges related to traveling in a society that segregated hotels and restaurants, and professional risks inherent in covering contentious events where danger loomed at every turn.

Newson, who escaped from a bus bombed outside Anniston, Alabama, during the Freedom Rides the year before, was stoic in recalling his decision to head to Oxford: "It was not a matter of being afraid, you recognize that some situations were quite dangerous... things happened when you doing that kind of work... You try to be cautious, you try to protect yourself, you try not to put yourself out in a situation leaving you open to special problems. If you were going to do it, you just did it."[180]

Newson said he headed to Oxford after receiving a telephone call from Jimmy Hicks, editor of the *Amsterdam News* in New York City. "When I heard that Meredith was going down to Ole Miss, man, I said, 'Well, if he goes, I'm gonna go, but it's dangerous country down there, you know.'"[181]

Hicks and Newson were longtime colleagues, having previously covered the integration of Central High School in Little Rock together and other breaking-news venues as civil rights stories exploded across the South. They met in Memphis at the photography studio of photographer Ernest Withers. Newson said: "On the highway on the way down vehicles were passing and going by with people waving, sounding as if they were going to a football game. Out there on that highway they were supporting the governor of Mississippi. There were lots of people volunteering to go down there. I saw it as a start of a new civil war, this guy was taking on the governor."[182] Later he recalled:

> For the record, we in the black press, we felt we needed to be there. We needed to be seen. A lot of the people involved were young kids. We needed to be out there and get what was going on... We weren't calling people agitators, or invading the south. We took the position that this is America, we are not foreigners, we can go from state to state without exactly being called outsiders.[183]

As the demonstration exploded into rioting, and because of the ban, the pair found a rooming house to spend the night. The next morning, Hicks was telling friendly white reporters about not being allowed to cover the story because of his race—ironically a mirror of the discrimination James Meredith himself had endured—when Oxford Police Chief Jimmy Jones wheeled into the parking lot at Oxford's Second Baptist Church and ordered the men to leave town.

They didn't leave. The pair hung around Oxford, interviewed residents and found sources who worked on campus to enliven their stories. Newson recalled, "Basically they were supporting what Meredith was doing, talking—to them around there was pretty much what we could do."[184]

> I had thought that after Little Rock, when Eisenhower called out the federal troops, that no one would have gone as far as they had in Mississippi. A standoff with the government? But when people go out to fight a civil war and die by the thousands in order to protest their superior view of their position in the world, that's serious. You can't laugh that off.[185]

Newson had covered the Emmett Till trial in 1955 and found Mississippi an intimidating place for a black reporter. Whites who challenged the status quo faced social and economic ruination, but blacks faced lynching and death. In the Deep South, to carry a press card and be branded an outsider was to wear a bull's-eye. In an interview for *Eyes on the Prize*, the award-winning PBS civil rights series, Hicks summed up the reality for black reporters:

> You must remember that there were blacks there all the time in the South, but it was danger because if you were gonna be a uppity nigger, as they called you down there, it was something, you were something that [was] a thorn in their side; and they would try to get rid of you by peaceful means, get out of town, or violent means, through the Klan or the citizens' clubs that they have down there. You would become discouraged if you didn't have stamina and guts.[186]

When Newson and Hicks covered the 1957 integration of Central High School in Little Rock, Arkansas, they—along with *Chicago*

Defender editor L. Alex Wilson and photographer Earl Davy—were attacked by a white mob.[187] The violence did not deter them but rather fueled their determination. The South was a rich source for stories that could have an impact on society.

> I think all the black reporters who covered those stories in the South knew that things could happen that would be harmful to them. I don't know, but I think the idea was to be as careful as you could, watch what you were doing and what others were doing about, and just try to protect yourself while you went about doing your job. Yeah, there were situations, not particularly in this case, but in other cases, where young people and older people were out fighting for their freedoms and equal opportunity that we all aspire to. So, it's a commitment to play a role in that kind of history.[188]

While black reporters were better able to gather information and develop sources in the black community, they had to deal with transportation, lodging and dining. Throughout the South, public facilities

THE COMPANY WILL APPRECIATE SUGGESTIONS FROM ITS PATRONS CONCERNING ITS SERVICE

CLASS OF SERVICE
This is a fast message unless its deferred character is indicated by the proper symbol.

WESTERN UNION
TELEGRAM
W. P. MARSHALL, PRESIDENT

SYMBOLS
DL=Day Letter
NL=Night Letter
LT=International Letter Telegram

1201 (4-60)

The filing time shown in the date line on domestic telegrams is LOCAL TIME at point of origin. Time of receipt is LOCAL TIME at point of destination

1962 SEP 27 AM 10 04

NSA024 SSA064

NS NA056 PD=NEW YORK NY 27 1114A EDT=

MARVIN BLACK=

DIRECTOR OF PUBLIC RELATIONS THE MISSISSIPPIAN

UNIVERSITY OF MISSISSIPPI OXFORD MISS=

I AM INFORMED THAT YOU HAVE REFUED ACCREDITDATION TO
JAMES L HICKS WHO IS ON ASSIGNMENT AND CANNOT COMPLETE
HIS JOB WILL YOU PLEASE RECONSIDER AND ACCREDIT THIS
REPORTER IN ORDER TO HAVE HIM FILE HIS STORY=

    JESSE WALKER CITY EDITOR NEW YORK AMSTERDAM NEWS.

Telegram courtesy University of Mississippi Archives

were segregated; budgets were tight at the small, under-funded black newspapers; buses often traveled over rural, isolated roads; and public officials were unlikely to provide assistance. Hicks recalled being warned before his first visit to Mississippi that "people down there, the white men down there, didn't think any more about killing a black man than they did about shooting a deer out of season."[189]

The black press during the civil rights era was, at times, more aggressive in covering segregation issues than the white press. Hank Klibanoff, co-author of *The Race Beat: The Press, the Civil Rights Struggle, and the Awakening of a Nation*, the comprehensive study of journalism and civil rights, said, "The black reporters were the first on the scene anywhere. They had a view of the black thought and the black community feeling about civil rights that white reporters did not venture in to find out."[190] This often caused reporters from the black press to stray from the narrow confines of traditional rules of objectivity. For Newson it was not so much a straying as finding a different voice:

Oxford Police Chief Jimmy Jones questioning Amsterdam News
executive editor James Hicks (far right).
Photo by Ed Meek.

83

The black press was born as a press too, as a media to do confrontation type of protests against the situation that we were living through at that time. We were quite supportive of changes, progress being made, and I think there was plenty of information out there about where the South stood. And of course, we did that to a certain extent. We interviewed people on both sides of issues, and we reported as best we could, as fairly as we could while it was taking place. I think to a greater extent, we sort of emphasized the subjugation; the problems that black people had, that they had to endure and we tried to bring, in an enforceable way, to the attention of the public.

We weren't concerned terribly about people saying we were unbalanced or that sort of thing. We thought the stories we did would stand up and stand a fair test of what they represented. But, we weren't really hung up on the idea that every time somebody said something on one side, we had to equate that to something else that was said on the other side. And quite frankly, this thing of fairness and balance often depends on what a person thinks, you know. What's balanced to you and what's objective to you may not be objective and fair to somebody else, so that's something to strive for in doing journalism work. And you have to do that, but at the same time, people often see things differently. We thought it was the role of the black press, to a certain extent; to make sure that the position of black people was out there so everybody could see and examine what their interests were.[191]

As the movement became more violent in the 1960s, the mainstream press began hiring black reporters. Editors needed minority staffers to cover the flood of civil rights stories swarming across the wires, national newspapers and networks. The result was a decline in the black press's circulation and leadership, but not its role.

Newson rose to editor of the *Afro-American*. He worked as a correspondent in post-civil war Nigeria and covered apartheid in South Africa. In 2008 he was inducted into the Hall of Fame of the Maryland-Delaware-District of Columbia Press Association.

OLE MISS IS WORSE THAN LITTLE ROCK

The Afro-American, October 6, 1962

by Moses J. Newson

Memphis, Tenn. - "I'll tell you, this is the worst I've seen and that includes Little Rock."

When Jimmy Hicks, executive editor of The Amsterdam News, gave me that wrap-up on Oxford, Miss., I knew things were rough.

Hicks and I have been hitting these racial hotspots together for years. We sweated the Till case trial together in Mississippi, welcomed the National Guard to Clinton, Tenn., together, and ran from the mob together at Little Rock, Arkansas.

When he missed the bus burning at Anniston, Ala., I got the feeling my old buddy had gone on the executive kick. But I knew Jimmy was back on the beat when my call from Memphis to Oxford roused him out of bed about 3 AM Friday, and he growled: "What are you waiting around up there for?"

He told me he'd been there since Tuesday, and no colored reporters were being allowed in the campus area "for our own safety."

I had been hearing about the problem from friendly white reporters. The mayor of Oxford had publicly suggested colored reporters stay home. Tom Dent, the NAACP publicity man for the Meredith case, said in a call from New Orleans that it might be better to stay out of Oxford.

While wrapping up some odds and ends Saturday, waiting for Meredith to come in from New Orleans, and getting me a tipster who could see when the Federal forces pulled out for Oxford, I heard a radio broadcast saying 200 armed Mobile, Ala., "volunteers" were en route to Oxford.

When I called Jimmy to tell him about this and my plans to slip in Sunday morning, he said: "Sit tight until you see me. I'm coming up for some fresh air."

Before I saw him, I heard why he was hitting the road.

He had finally worked his way onto the campus. The [state troopers] refused to admit him though and suggested he get out of town.

That wasn't enough for ole Jimmy though. He went back to his stopping place and had started granting an interview to some white reporters who had followed him, when three police cars wheeled in.

To make it short, they broke up the press conference, and Police Chief Jimmy Jones suggested Hicks could be charged with trespassing on the Ole Miss campus and with inciting to riot by holding a press conference on city property in the colored neighborhood.

Police chief Jones suggested Jimmy get out of Oxford.

That was it. Two trips a day to the campus since Tuesday where troopers curtly ordered him away. Then the police chief. Jimmy hit the road.

That's how we happened to be together in Memphis, waiting for Meredith to come in, and trying to figure out a better way to cover the doings in Oxford.

FLIP SCHULKE

Photographer Flip Schulke spent part of the night of September 30, 1962 crouching in the bushes surrounding the Circle. Schulke, who was shooting his first assignment for *Life* magazine in Oxford, would go on to even greater fame covering civil rights stories, many featuring the Rev. Martin Luther King Jr. But for the kid from New Ulm, Minnesota, Oxford was almost too much.

I'm 6 foot 3. I was skinny... stood sidewise, and you couldn't hit me. But, yeah, I was scared. I mean, I've never been shot at. Later, some of the guys that came back from Vietnam and Korea said it was worse there [in Oxford] because your own people were shooting at you. It was kind of like the Army would shoot their own people because they didn't know who was in front of them, but it was very, very dangerous. I'm hiding. I'm certainly not gonna use flash. I mean, I had four kids. I wanted to survive and I knew damn well that if I hit a flash off I didn't know how many people were on those buildings.[192]

Schulke gained entrance to the campus by hiding under a blanket in the backseat of a car driven by a professor he had met on a previous visit. "I gave him a ring and said the highway patrol had ringed the campus at every one of the entrances and all over, and they were letting every segregationist in with rifles and everything and keeping all the newsmen off."[193]

He was in the right place to shoot the iconic photograph of the Lyceum—directly in front of the marshals as dusk descended. "I didn't have a tear gas mask on but I was able to get some pictures and then I went in the bushes because it's really hard with that tear gas. Luckily, it wasn't the newer type which makes you throw up, but you can't see." [194]

While taking shelter in the bushes, he heard footsteps and shouted out a warning to Paul Guihard. "I yelled, get down and this French accent came back at me, saying, 'I'm not worried, I was in Cyprus.' I will always remember that because I didn't know much about Cyprus, but [Ole Miss] was a dangerous place."[195]

The Oxford Square, October 1
© *Flip Schulke*

At that point, Schulke decided to head back to the *Life* command center at his motel.

"I wasn't there [when Guihard was murdered]. I was in the bushes, but then I left. I snuck off. They weren't worried about you coming off, they were worried about you getting on," he added. "This was my first experience, personal experience with the danger and violence."[196]

Later, when he heard of Guihard's death, it finally dawned on Schulke how dangerous the situation had become: "The camera is like a wall between you and danger, and you take chances. I had never been under fire before. You wonder if it is worth it... I reached a point where I decided that if I was going to risk my life, it had to be for something I truly, deeply believed in."[197]

His moment of truth came several years later, but had its roots in his childhood experience with an abusive father who was anti-Semitic [even though his wife was part Jewish] and racist. Raised in a wealthy family with a black cook, Schulke was exposed to economic contrasts and rigid social lines, "Our black cook became a surrogate mother to me. Black people were not only in the house, but they brought their children. I always found it easy to get along with them. I learned at a very early age that you judge somebody not on their color or their religion, but on who they are."[198]

But the idyllic life of winters in Florida came crashing to an end after the Internal Revenue Service came after his father for unpaid taxes. Living in the winter of 1945 in an unheated cabin in Cornish, New Hampshire, and keeping the fire in the furnace going all night, Schulke was forced to drop out of school. At age 15, unable to deal with an increasingly belligerent alcoholic father, Schulke left for New Ulm in 1946.[199] His grandmother and uncle lived in New Ulm, and the city became for him a logical, if temporary, retreat. His situation quickly turned dire when his grandmother died and his uncle was diagnosed with dementia.

Penniless, he shined shoes, worked as a dishwasher and cook, and began taking photographs with a Baby Brownie camera, roughly 2.5 inches square. His photography for the local newspaper was an overnight success, enabling Schulke to buy a car and a Speed Graphic, the classic box camera used by press photographers.[200] Housing fluctuated, from the attic of his grandmother's apartment building to the basement of the same building to the home of the high school football coach. This skittish existence contributed to his desire to document wrongs imposed on the underdog.

Schulke went to Macalester College. His interest in photography stemmed not from talent or the joy of taking photographs, but to make a living. At Macalester, he fell under the tutelage of Ivan Burg, a former photo editor for the *St. Paul Pioneer Press*, and his career path was set. Later, Wilson Hicks, a former photo editor for The Associated Press, mentored Schulke, who quickly developed the ability to capture the story with a single, unforgettable image: "I saw the unfair way blacks were being treated, and I couldn't stand the intolerance. I believed in America. We had just gone through the Second World War when we were fighting for freedom, freedom for all people. I was very influenced by Lewis Hine, who did photographs of child labor. I wanted to be like the writers who exposed injustice."[201] Schulke developed and refined a photographer's most important talent:

> The big thing about being a photographer, versus a writer, is that a photographer must be on the spot where the action is going to happen before it happens. Newspaper reporters, many times, are also there when the action happens, but they can go down later to ask questions. Photographers can't do that. You either get the photo when the action happens or you don't. I had the ability to anticipate events, but it wasn't a psychic ability. I questioned everything.[202]

Schulke began covering the Rev. Martin Luther King Jr. in 1958. It was that relationship that enabled Schulke to understand his role as a photojournalist. As Schulke tells the story, he was covering the civil rights struggles in Selma, Alabama, in 1965, when he saw children attacked by police and various protestors. Without thinking, he pushed a club away from a policeman. King took Schulke aside and said: "Flip, you did wrong. I can understand you losing your temper, but unless you record what happened, the world won't know that child got beaten... Your job is to photograph what is happening to us. You can't be a participant."[203] It was that difference that first drew him to the field: "In all the years I had been working, no one had so clearly spelled out the difference between observing history and being a participant. The important thing was to illustrate what you saw happening so that people would understand better by seeing your pictures." [204]

Despite offers from the nation's leading magazines, Schulke was never a photo staffer.

He worked freelance because it enabled him to retain ownership of his photographs. He worked for *Life, Time, Ebony, Sports Illustrated, Newsweek, National Geographic* and *Look*. His list of photo subjects includes Muhammad Ali, Jacques Cousteau, Fidel Castro, Elvis Presley and eight U.S. presidents. He was one of the first photographers inside the Texas School Book Depository after President John F. Kennedy's assassination.

After his experience shooting photographs that night in Oxford, desperate not to attract the attention of rioters, Schulke developed a strobe with deep red filters that enabled nighttime photography without a sharp flash of white light.[205] The strobe became a classic in the field.

Winner of multiple awards from the National Press Photographers Association, Schulke donated his collection of more than 600,000 images to the Briscoe Center for American History, The University of Texas at Austin, in 1999. Approximately 10,000 of the photographs document Rev. King and the civil rights movement.

The Lyceum, September 30.
© *Flip Schulke*

Photo courtesy University of Mississippi Archives.

SIDNA BROWER

The school year had barely begun when Sidna Brower, the new editor of *The Mississippian*, the Ole Miss student newspaper, was covering a murder, reporting on a riot and facing censure for her editorials calling for good behavior on campus.

It was a formidable task for the Memphis native, sorority girl and journalism major but she accomplished it with professionalism, grace and the support of her family and professors. In addition, Brower's editorials calling for calm were nominated for a Pulitzer Prize and she received accolades from professional journalists around the country in the form of editorials, awards and job offers.

Brower was not alone among university editors in the South who faced down their peers and took positions related to segregation.

Her case is unique because she never advocated for integration and, while the desegregation of other universities across the South was contentious, campus opposition did not rise to the level of a riot, nor was the U.S. Army needed to enforce federal court orders. The student government censure stood for 40 years before it was rescinded with apologies.

Brower, who went on to own a weekly newspaper in Denville, N.J., admits that as the school year started she was more focused on getting the student newspaper on sound financial footing than ground-breaking journalism. The previous spring, in a campus-wide election, she was elected editor of the school paper after serving as a news editor. She assembled a staff and covered the Meredith story as it evolved.

The students were less concerned with the looming integration crisis than with their classes, social events and football games when they returned to campus that fall. Classes started a week earlier and according to Brower, most students were apolitical. Because the legal battles were conducted in courtrooms several hundred miles away Meredith's quest appeared abstract and his enrollment unlikely.

That didn't stop her from reporting on developments, or from giving the national media access to *The Mississippian's* darkroom and typewriters in its Brady Hall offices about a quarter-mile from the Lyceum throughout the month.

The night of the riot, reporters also used Brady Hall as a sanctuary from the tear gas. "Their eyes were horrible. They would come in and their eyes were burning and they were crying. We would get paper towels and towels and clean their eyes and wash their faces and then they'd go back out," recalled Kay Veasey, who worked as a typist in the newsroom as an Oxford High School student.[206]

Long-distance lines were few in Oxford and Veasey, who went on to major in journalism at Ole Miss, said that staffers kept a line open for the *Memphis Commerical Appeal* personnel using their newsroom throughout the night. Her father walked from his nearby home to check on her at one point, but had no objections to her remaining in Brady Hall. "I was 17 years old and I certainly didn't realize it was going to even be talked about. I was very surprised to see it was on the national news and that the Kennedy's knew anything about it," Veasey added.[207]

Brower's idealistic view of the professionalism of the national media, meanwhile, was shattered earlier in the month when a broadcast reporter called on a crowd of students to perform so he would have film. One student climbed the campus flagpole bearing a Confederate flag. Brower was appalled: "In a way, [it was] big news to show what idiots we were in Mississippi."[208]

The experience later fueled her career as the owner of the weekly *Citizen*: "I became, as a journalist, a young one, cynical, and I guess I remained that way. I wanted my reporters to make sure that they were indeed reporting it and not forcing an issue."[209] For Brower, accumulating the facts, searching for the truth in the evidence, and providing context were the hallmarks of a journalist, not creating the news.

Brower arrived on campus shortly after Meredith moved into Baxter Hall. Like many students, she attended the Ole Miss - Kentucky football game in Jackson the day before. For the first time at an Ole Miss football game Confederate flags furnished by the White Citizens Council were distributed. At halftime, stadium lights were dimmed for a candlelight ceremony exalting the "Southern way of life." Gov. Ross Barnett brought the fans to their feet with a brief, emotional speech: "My fellow Mississippians, I love Mississippi. I love her people, our customs. I love and respect our heritage." For Brower, Barnett's glorification by students and alumni was strange and worrisome: "This was a governor who couldn't even come to the Ole Miss campus, to ballgames, because tomatoes would be thrown at him. All of a sudden, he was a hero, and people were rolling with Ross."[210]

Barnett's implied appeal to "save Ole Miss" from integration rippled across the state. On Sunday, WLBT-TV in Jackson called on concerned citizens to rendezvous in Oxford and resist Meredith's admission. Brower and her date had spent the night at his parents' home. Alarmed by the news on the radio, her date's father begged them not to return to campus. Brower insisted that, as editor of the newspaper, she had a responsibility to prepare the next day's edition. Her escort's father strenuously objected, deeming it "unsafe for a woman," but Brower prevailed, and along with hundreds of other students returned to Oxford by mid-afternoon.

Only one staffer out of 22 (including sports, entertainment and society sections) was unable to make it to the newsroom. Brower recalled that the staffer spent the early evening dressed in a Confederate uniform until his National Guard unit was called to duty. "Someone threw a railroad tie down off the trestle onto his jeep, which I guess hit the hood or something. He said, 'At that point, I became an American,'" she said.[211]

On campus, she phoned staff members to meet her at the *Mississippian* office and began preparing for a special edition.[212] Not only did the paper have a deadline but Brower and her female staff members were facing an 11 p.m. curfew requiring them to be in their residence halls. The dean of women had warned them that they would be penalized if they failed to do so.

Brower went into the Circle expecting an orderly demonstration only to be confronted by burning cars and tear gas. "I was shocked to see the Lyceum surrounded by federal marshals. They were standing there, really elbow to elbow. How they stood there as long as they did, I don't know. I was walking around to try to view what was happening, and listening to some of the chants, when a Molotov cocktail shattered at my feet, fortunately, it didn't go off, but I realized, this was like war."[213]

Who were these wild young men running through the Grove, hurling bricks and lead pipes at the federal marshals, beating up reporters and setting cars on fire? Her world, her university, everything she believed in, had been turned upside down. She searched the faces of the shadowy figures rushing by in the smoke-filled darkness. "Some were students but some of them obviously were not. I told one boy: 'Why don't you go home?' and I took bottles and eggs away from others."[214]

Mississippi state troopers slouched around, barely making an effort to control the crowd, and seldom interfering with random attacks on newsmen. Stan Opotowsky of *The New York Post* vividly captured the scene:

> A boy student held an empty soft drink bottle in his hand, leaned back in perfect pitching stance and then called to his confederates, 'Y'all get ready to run.' He heaved the bottle and it crashed to the street at the feet of a U.S. marshal. Four marshals spun around and fired their guns: poppety, pop, pop, pow. There were flashes of light, and then the white smoke of tear gas and the students ran and stumbled and hurdled a fence in a headlong flight from the stinging fumes.[215]

Brower "was so furious when she saw what was going on," wrote *Memphis Press-Scimitar* journalist Dickson Preston, "she marched into her office and wrote an editorial telling off the rioters in cold and stinging type."[216]

Fearing that her staff might be attacked, Brower locked the newsroom's outer doors. "All of these people were coming in who were certainly outsiders. You could see the hatred and hear it in their voices."[217]

At some point between 9 p.m., when Paul Guihard was murdered, and 11 p.m., Brower was sharing the Brady Hall darkroom with Sammy Schulman, Guihard's photographer. There was a knock on the door. A visitor called through the closed door that a reporter had been shot near the Fine Arts building. Brower recalled: "I don't remember whether I asked, 'Who?' or whether the person said it was Paul Guihard, the French correspondent. The photographer said, 'Oh my God! That's my man,' and he left to go see what had happened and, I guess, ultimately, claim the body."[218]

Shocked and chastened, Brower finished putting the newspaper to bed, and then returned to the Kappa Kappa Gamma sorority house. Crossing the campus, she came under fire. "It was a very disturbing night," she recalled. "There were bullets still flying."[219] A UPI photographer escorted her to the Kappa house. "We could hear shots. It felt like, or seemed like, a bullet had gone right in front of us. Thank goodness the photographer was with me, because I don't know what I would have done without him."[220]

97

Distribution of the newspaper at the scheduled time of 5 a.m., ordinarily a routine matter, was interrupted when the student advertising manager, a segregationist, refused to deliver the newspaper.[221] Brower enlisted the help of a Phi Delta fraternity friend and a reporter from *The Christian Science Monitor* to help her com-

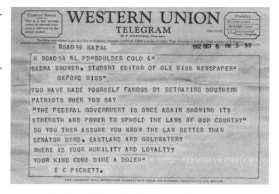

Courtesy University of Mississippi Archives.

plete the deliveries. Students woke up to find the paper in the dorms, sorority and fraternity houses containing candid reports of the riot, as well as Sidna's courageous editorial denouncing the use of violence. [222]

The front page contained a report of the violence and a photograph of U.S. marshals in front the Lyceum.[223] The headline read: "Chancellor Issues Plea; Death, injuries from campus rioting."[224] Many readers were enraged by Brower's editorial calling for moderation and law and order. She received hate mail and anonymous threats, and ultimately was censured by the student government.

The editorial: "The Violence Will Not Help" was an appeal to the student body to behave without rancor. It was this editorial, and others calling out the campus community for bad behavior, which led to the censure resolution. "I really never came right out and said I'm for integration. It was really a tense time. In assessing the situation, I felt that just might add fuel to the fire," she said.[225] She took no position on Meredith's admission even though she supported it. Rather, it was a reflection of her arrival on campus after attending the football game Saturday, and returning to campus to find it in turmoil. "I didn't think taking a position [on integration] would help any," Brower said. "Southerners are normally respectful of the law, and that's what I appealed to."[226]

Brower soon learned who were her friends and who were her enemies: "Two [sorority sisters] who were at the top of the main stairs didn't like what I had written, and one would spit on me if I went up the front stairs. My room was on one of the wings so I soon learned, just go up the back stairs and avoid that. Years later at a Kappa reunion, the other girl apologized to me and said she was wrong in the way she treated me." [227]

The morning after the riot on her way to Brady Hall, Brower passed through three military checkpoints. She walked past the Lyceum, observing the horrendous damage done to the bucolic campus. No one sneered at her. Instead, many praised her editorial.[228] The glow did not last.

By midmorning the next day, critical, angry and disturbing letters, postcards and telegrams started pouring in, scorning her for the paper's coverage, and her editorial. The letters were written on engraved paper, on paper torn from spiral notebooks and squeezed onto notepad paper. Some were typed with professionalism, others were written in scrawls hard to read because of the elaborate handwriting, bad spelling or absence of basic grammatical skills. Hundreds were sent between October 1 and the end of the school year. They fill three legal boxes in the university archives.

The letters carried with them common threads, that Brower had turned her back on her race, her peers on campus and Southern standards; she had fallen prey to the unlawful acts of the Kennedys in her innocence; or she was building her career. A woman from Vicksburg, Mississippi, wrote: "First, may I ask if you are part African? Next, are you being subsidized by the NAACP or some other communistic dominated organization?" [229]

These sentiments were echoed in a telegram sent from Boulder, Colorado, with the writer condemning Brower for "betraying Southern patriots" and asking, "where is your humility and loyalty?" A woman from Gadsden, Alabama, called Brower "a rotten apple" and suggested she and Meredith "transfer to a college that suits you better. If you are pretty, it's pretty ugly. This should cut you down to your size in the opinion of every blue blooded American in the

United States." Another woman, writing from New Orleans, took the position "as a mother and Grand mother" to write: "As a white woman, your first duty is to preserve the purity and future integrity of the white race, and you should be prepared to sacrifice your life for this holy purpose."[230]

Not all the mail was negative. A lead editorial in the *San Francisco Chronicle* praised Brower: "In its comments on the Meredith case, the student paper at the University of Mississippi has shown more good sense and principle than the Governor, the Legislature, the bar and most of the rest of the Mississippi press.... It takes some courage for a young editor to stand up to the yowls of a mob and the mummery of the authorities in a racially inflamed situation, more especially when the editor is a young woman. We pay our respects to Editor Brower of the Mississippian."[231]

The letters did not stop her from writing editorials calling on students to accept Meredith's presence after incidents of harassment directed toward him, or to students who attempted to befriend him.

The incidents included having their belongings ransacked and bleach poured on their clothes when they returned to their dorms. Brower responded in her column that students had the right to associate with anyone they wished. "It doesn't mean you have to, but as a university, we should have that freedom," she wrote, later recalling, "I'd say that stirred up some folks that felt that I wasn't upholding Southern traditions."[232]

Slurs and insults, and a student protest to have her removed as editor, did not keep her from writing editorials, nor did it halt the paper's goal of providing the Ole Miss community with the facts. Brower recognized the power of the press to help people understand events and to place them in the larger context of community involvement, even if those events shamed the university. She also had a passion for the university and its image to the outside world. Brower recalled:

> I had gone out to the airport when the soldiers were landing, and it was just an incredible sight to walk along the runway and see soldiers lined up on the side as far as you could see. To have

the planes come in and the troops and other equipment come out, and you're thinking, this is the University of Mississippi and all of these soldiers are there. What does this do to our campus? They gradually kind of disappeared, but it was still sort of holding over our heads that we were occupied.[233]

The troops remained for about a week, gradually withdrawing as tensions eased and the troublemakers went back to their homes. Military police accompanied Meredith until his graduation in August. James Silver, a history professor and activist frequently quoted by the national media, advised Brower not to interview Meredith. He was concerned that, as a white female, she might cause problems for herself and Meredith.[234]

Silver, who had his own controversial relationship with the university, was the author of *Mississippi: The Closed Society*, which condemned the state's political and business leaders for their insular attitudes before and during the crisis.[235] Brower, who maintained a lifelong correspondence with Silver after they both left Mississippi, heeded his advice, agreeing that the criticism she faced was enough without giving her critics more ammunition.

> Just seeing what occurred when people ate with [Meredith] at lunch, and already people were not happy with my editorials, that that would just create more problems. I know that there was a radio station, I think out of Jackson, that was claiming again I was a n----- lover and that I was sleeping with James Meredith and all of this. My father had gotten wind of this and went to a lawyer and asked about suing. The lawyer said, "It's not worth it. Just let it go."[236]

It had not been easy, she recalled, to get to know Meredith when they were students. "He couldn't just stop and get a Coke while walking across campus. He always had marshals [guarding him] and people screaming derogatory things at him."[237] During a 40th anniversary program, she approached Meredith and expressed her regret for not interviewing him in 1962. He revealed that Professor Silver had also advised him not to speak to Brower "for my own safety." Meredith reminded her of his letter to *The Mississippian* explaining his position, a letter which, Brower said, she had been delighted to publish.[238]

In response to her editorials, an anonymous broadside called *The Rebel Underground* labeled Brower "the Pink Princess" and launched a campaign to have her removed.[239] Kappa Alpha fraternity tried to impeach her. The campus committee on student rights and activities voted to reprimand her. The motion called for her to apologize for her editorials or resign.[240] She did not apologize nor did she resign. "I really never came right out and said 'I'm for integration.' It was really a tense time. In assessing the situation, I felt that it just might add fuel to the fire," she said.[241]

In late November of 1962, a senate member of a Citizens Council youth group introduced a resolution to censure Brower. When the motion failed, she was reprimanded with a motion contending she "failed in a time of grave crisis to uphold the rights of students."[242] The senators changed the wording from censure to reprimand because they were fearful that censure would be read as censor and they wanted to avoid any misunderstanding regarding their intent.

The censure resolution only hinted at the content of her editorials. Instead, the complainants argued that Brower didn't editorialize in favor for their position and thus, she failed "to uphold the rights of students." The student Senate sought editorials in favor of "Southern traditions."[243]

Brower noted, however, "They couldn't really explain what they meant by southern traditions."[244] Instead, Brower said her editorials were such that she wrote: "You don't have to eat with James Meredith, but don't ostracize those willing to do so. This is a university, and people are free to express their opinion."[245]

In her letter to the Senate as part of the process, Brower chided the senators that they were also elected by the students and were obligated to represent all the students, adding:

> Most of these editorial comments have carried the theme of denouncing violence... What are you condemning? Are you saying that the riots were something to be proud of and this violence should be continued?... The only demonstrations against Meredith's presence here have been destructive . . .You want to censor the editor because she supported the right for a student

to associate with a persons or persons of his choice and the right to say what he believes. And yet you say you would deny these rights to any students.[246]

As part of the proceeding, the senators wanted to see the letters received in *The Mississippian* offices, contending the ones Brower chose to publish did not represent the majority views of the letter writers. Lacking adequate space in the newsroom, Brower had taken them home to Memphis, an hour and a half away northwest in Tennessee. The letters filled three garbage bags. Proceedings were halted until Brower produced the letters.

The senate was also informed by Brower that she would continue to editorialize as she felt appropriate: "They can certainly do me no harm for I shall continued to write what I feel is just and right and that in which I desperately hope most of the students believe."[247]

Brower was stunned by the reprimand. "I was basically trying to say, 'Don't riot. Don't bring shame to the university.'"[248]

> I was admittedly careful in the editorials, and even the fact that I mentioned Ross Barnett, in one, of trying to appeal to people who might have been coming there with some pretty bad motives. Although I personally believed that James Meredith had a right to be there, I knew if I said that, that it would cause more problems for me, and for him, and no one would listen to either one of us.[249]

The resolution attached additional stigma to the campus, and the national press covered the debate even as the senators took three hours to decide if network cameras and national newsmen were welcome in the meeting.[250]

"As it turned out, I got a lot of positive press all over the world, but unfortunately the censure reflected poorly on the university," she recalled."[251] "A number of newspapers really blasted the students for what they did to me."[252] In contrast, the administration and faculty supported her editorials as a voice of reason, she said.[253]

The censure stood until 2002. During ceremonies marking the 40th anniversary of the university's integration, the Senate rescinded the censure. "It was the right thing to do," said Will Bardwell, the

Senate's communications director, "In 1962, the truth was not what everybody wanted to hear."[254]

"It really touched me deeply," Brower said, after learning of the resolution in an email. "For the first few years (after graduating), it was something that haunted me. That really shook me up."[255]

The arch-conservative Mississippi Sovereignty Commission, a state-funded agency that monitored civil rights activity, also demanded an explanation. "I got called out of a history class during exams, and I had to go to the Alumni House, or to the conference room. There were all of these old white-to me, old white men-sitting around a table," she recalled.[256] "I look back now and say I should have had a lawyer or should have had somebody there. But I felt like, hey, I have nothing to hide. I can answer their questions... The sad part was when I went back to finish my exam, the professor would not allow me to continue taking the exam. I had to take a different exam on another day."[257]

A search of the Sovereignty Commission files housed in the Mississippi Department of Archives and History turned up five newspaper articles that mentioned Brower. The stories focused on her editorials and the censure movement. No report of the interview could be found. No individual file exists on Brower. The files located were housed in Meredith's file, a much larger series of folders.[258]

Because of her public stance, her father's dairy business in Memphis sustained losses, but her parents remained staunchly supportive.[259] Brower recalled that her father told her: "Don't worry about it. You write what you think is right."

> Growing up, he was the one who, at the dinner table, when we would discuss about what was going on in the world, he would say, "You don't judge a person by where they live, what their religion is, or the color of their skin." My mother, who is from Mississippi, would always say, "Well, what about the poor American Indians?" Which is true, but that was not the case. I guess my father was a lot more liberal than my mother. He was from Kentucky.[260]

Years later, while cleaning out storage boxes from her family home she found letters from some of his father's customers: "They were basically saying, 'We agree with what Sidna said, but we can't say that publicly because of our business.'"[261]

As to the Pulitzer Prize nomination, Francis Stuart Harmon, a former secretary of the state's higher education board, nominated Brower. Harmon, in his nomination letter, wrote: "From first-hand experience, I know something of the pressures to which Miss Brower is now being subjected. Moral support and special recognition tends to strengthen those, who, in last analysis, must change the climate of opinion."[262] Harmon lost his position on the state board when he opposed former Gov. Theodore Bilbo, who sought to reorganize the state's institutions of higher learning for political purposes. Harmon went on to serve as general secretary of the International Commission of the YMCA, vice president of the Motion Picture Association of America, and vice president of the Interchurch Center in New York City.

Brower did not win the Pulitzer Prize but has no regrets: " I prayed that I would not get it. Can you imagine at twenty-one? Where would you go?"[263]

Brower's career was just beginning. *Mademoiselle* selected her as one of ten national merit winners. She landed internships in New York with the *World-Telegram* and in London with United Press International. Later she worked for Citibank in employee communications, then as a hospital community affairs director, and in development for a management-consulting firm. In addition to co-publishing the *Citizen,* she served as deputy director of the New Jersey Council on Affordable Housing in Trenton and became active in politics.

Photo by Ed Meek.

THE VIOLENCE WILL NOT HELP

The Mississippian, October 1, 1962

By Sidna Brower

This is an appeal to the entire student body and to anyone concerned with the present situation. Not only do the students chance forfeiting their education by participating in riots, but they are bringing dishonor and shame to the University and the State of Mississippi.

When students hurled rocks, bottles, and eggs the federal marshals were forced to resort to tear gas to back off the crowds.

When outsiders show their objections in the form of violence, they are seriously injuring the students in their attempt to continue their education. As a student, I beg you to return to your homes.

This is a battle between the State of Mississippi and the United States government; the University is caught in the middle. The Civil War was fought over one hundred years ago over almost the same issues and the United States of America prevailed. The federal government is once again showing its strength and power to uphold the laws of our country.

No matter what your convictions, you should follow the advice of Governor Ross Barnett by not taking any action for violence. Blood has already been shed and will continue to flow unless people realize the seriousness of the situation.

Whatever your beliefs, you are a citizen of the United States of America and of the State of Mississippi, and should preserve peace and harmony of both governments.

Courtesy of Fred Powledge.

FRED POWLEDGE

Fred Powledge of *The Atlanta Journal* narrowly escaped three beatings during the night of September 30. When he asked for assistance from the state police, they passively stood by, leaving Powledge with the distinct impression that state police were not interested in controlling the crowd, or in helping the press.

Powledge, who had driven to Oxford with Bill Shipp of the *Atlanta Constitution*, said they, and all other reporters who had not been able to find an alternative route to campus, were detained from entering the campus by the state police until about 7 p.m. when the barriers were removed: "The reporters were all hemmed in, agitating, and tapping our hooves on the ground because we wanted to get in there, up to the administration building. They didn't let us do that."[264]

Powledge recalled, that as the press corps left the Hildgard bridge, he noticed that the state police were almost jovial: "As they left, some of them were grinning. And I wondered why. Later on I found out." [265] The press corps headed for the Lyceum.

"When the bottleneck (at the bridge) was removed pretty much everybody raced up the oval. The way the federal marshals were lined up, it was pretty obvious that was where the action was."[266] He called the decision "letting sheep in for the slaughter."[267]

The reporters found a campus awash in roaming people, some students, some adults from the county, and an increasing number of people from outside the area intent on thwarting the enrollment of Meredith through violence. *Life* magazine photographer Charles Moore recalled:

> Some of the racist students and some pretty tough guys, football players and all that, were not on the side of the press. One guy who was with his friends was just a little bit bigger. He came up to me and started cursing me. He got mad at me and I told him to leave me alone and, no, he was not going to break my camera over my head. So he took his rebel flag and he brought it down and jabbed it against my camera. I pulled away and said you do that again you'll get the camera over your head. He cursed me, next thing, we were photographing someone important, and what I did when he was hitting me with the flagstaff; you know, [that] have those little arrows on it. He was jabbing me in the chest, just enough to hurt, I put my camera in my left hand and I took my right hand and brought it down and [the flagstaff] broke."[268]

There were reports of damaged press vehicles, destroyed cameras and a general feeling that the night was going to get really ugly. It also became obvious to the reporters that the crowd appeared to harbor hatred of the newsmen and marshals, and that a riot was about to explode. Powledge and Shipp separated as they were not working as a team, but they did make an effort to watch out for each other. While competitive when getting the story, they were not about to let each other down when violence erupted.

Powledge recalled that while taking photographs of the interaction between students and federal marshal in front of the Lyceum, he was approached by a neatly dressed student who asked: "Are you one of those nigger-loving reporters." He replied briskly, with a hint of his own North Carolina accent that did no good "as the young man hit me, aiming for my chin, I'm quite certain, but landing on my arm which I put up to defend myself, and he started in again with his other fist and hit me on the chest."[269] "It wasn't serious, I didn't go down. Bill Ship was there and kind of rescued me, saying let's get out of here."[270]

At the time men and boys were scurrying about, collecting bricks and soda bottles to use as missiles, calling out battle cries and rebel yells. The languid Sunday afternoon had turned into a night with sharp edges. Gene Sherman of *The Los Angeles Times* compared the scene to "a picnic on a volcano."[271] For Powledge it was a barometer of what to come:

> I saw more than one, and I suppose, less than four state police-men watching this incident. I remember distinctly seeing at least one of them grin. They were obviously not going to come to my aid. They were obviously going to do nothing but be spectators. I had the feeling that they would have entered this altercation, only if I had been on the winning side... I should add here that these policemen whom I saw were about 15 feet from me.[272]

The job of the state police was to keep the students separate from the U.S. Marshals.
Photo by Ed Meek

It was around 8 p.m. when the second attack occurred, at about the same time the violence escalated from spiteful yelling and the tossing of small stones and firecrackers to hurling metal pipes and Molotov cocktails. Before giving the order to use tear gas, Chief Marshal James McShane met with Col. T.B. Birdsong, head of the state police, seeking to secure greater cooperation. The conversation was fraught with political overtones. Birdsong told him Gov. Barnett was going to withdraw the state police from campus. McShane said, "I recall him very vividly saying to us that it was all right for me to insist that we cooperate, but he said, and I am now quoting him, 'We have to live there long after you people are gone.'"[273]

Accompanied by state Sen. George Yarbrough, Barnett's representative on campus, Birdsong then walked out to address the crowd. Some 1,000 students and outsiders had breached the truck barricade in front of the Lyceum. McShane, watching from the portico, noted:

I saw quite a number of police, but there was no police line. Then police were mixed in with the crowd and in some instances I saw the heads of some of the police officers back at the sixth or seventh row talking and mingling with the crowd, smiling and nodding, but making no effort to try to control this crowd or trying to get them under proper supervision. I watched what Col. Birdsong would do. He did not speak to any police officer, or rather to any uniformed police officer.[274]

At that point, McShane said one of the command deputy marshals handed him a lead pipe about two feet long which had been thrown at the marshals. The crowd had pushed into the top of The Circle. McShane looked around. The Department of Justice officials holed up in the Lyceum had left the decision to him to use tear gas or firearms should the need arise.

I decided that there was one of two ways for the deputy marshals to take charge of the situation. One way was for me to give an order to walk forward and use physical force to push the crowd back and start to control it by using force to disperse the crowd. However, I knew that this method would involve physical combat with the result that people on both sides would be injured—possibly seriously. The other method was to use the tear gas equipment we had. By doing this there would be no physical contact with the crowd and the crowd would surely be dispersed without any injury.[275]

McShane noted that the crowd appeared to be "sneering" at Yarbrough, ignoring his words, and that the state police were not assisting him. "I made up my mind the situation was not going to get any better and could only get worse. So I gave the order to fire. I did not have my gas mask on. The gas started to drift back. It got in my eyes. I went into the Lyceum to clear my eyes."[276]

Powledge heard McShane order the marshals to fire tear gas into the mob that had rapidly swelled to 2,000 people: "Let'em have it! Gas!" The goal was to disperse the crowd and create a secure perimeter for the U.S. Marshals. "I can't tell you possibly how tense the situation was during the afternoon," Powledge said in a recent interview, adding he had no doubts that he was in the middle of a major story. "The excitement of the event, the seriousness of the event, here was the first known black student admitted to the University of Mississippi, which was quite mildly did not have a good reputation in terms of race relations. Meredith really pissed them off to a great extent and that was transferred to us who witnessed his entry."[277]

For Marshal Felix M. Aycock, 29, of San Francisco, the man who fired the first tear gas container, the order to fire tear gas was welcomed by the marshals: "It seemed like an eternity that we waited. We should have fired sooner. The rocks were getting bigger and bigger. The crowd was throwing rocks, bricks, gravel, eggs, bottles."[278] The exploding canisters filled the air with a blinding mist. The crowd screamed and retreated.[279]

Powledge noted that before the first tear gas was fired, the marshals raised their weapons in the air in warning. "The mob shouted almost in unison, 'Watch out! They're going to use tear gas.'" According to Powledge "The press needed all the defense we could get" as the situation rapidly escalated further into violence and mayhem.[280]

The first grenade, I believe, was of the circular, bouncing, projectile type, and it was fired, it seems to me, at a rather low trajectory. I knew that the grenades would go quite far if they were fired at a certain angle. This first grenade seemed to be a warning. The students, again I must correct myself, the mob, probably felt the same way. They scattered. They ran back. There was a small stampede. I noticed many, not many, but a good portion, a good number of the people, a number I could not estimate, just kept on running and got off this little grove at this point. These, I figured, were the people who were willing to go along with the thing as long as it was fun to them . . .But when the tear gas came out they were ready to go home . . .But the hard core... it stopped, gathered itself and advanced again on the marshals. The marshals waited, I believe, a good long while before firing the second round... My feelings were that they wanted people to know that they were willing to use the tear gas. . . .

The crowd advanced again and again on the marshals. Got very close at one point. Threw more bottles, more bricks. The temper of the yelling increased and the insults became particularly vile at this point . . .This was the point where the words "motherfucker" were being used almost in a steady stream . . .

The marshals then used tear gas again, and I would place this second firing at maybe as much as five minutes after the first round. They used several rounds . . .Three, four or five at this point, but still firing from a scrimmage line in front of the building. The students ran back again and regrouped.[281]

The order to use tear gas came moments before President John F. Kennedy took to the airwaves, informing the nation that the campus was calm.

Reports were mixed over whether or not the crowd was aware Meredith was on campus, safely ensconced in his dormitory room a half-mile away, or if fear of his pending arrival stoked the crowd's actions. The rioters' anger focused on the Lyceum because Deputy Attorney General Nicholas Katzenbach had placed them there as a visible presence of federal authority. The sight of the federal marshals wearing new bright white helmets and armed with batons (and some with sidearms) reminded many of the Civil War when the union army occupied the Lyceum. The protestors were fighting for their ancestors.

And the riot was on.

Richard Russell, a junior at Ole Miss who later became a medical doctor, recalled: "I keenly remember witnessing the Lyceum ringed with fully geared-up U S. marshals who were taunting the gathering crowd of students. We were not aware of President Kennedy's famous TV speech calling for 'calm,' but did realize later that, shortly after his speech, the marshals suddenly lowered their tear gas canister guns and fired directly into the crowd of students. Several were severely hurt by the canisters."[282]

Tear gas forced the crowd away from the Lyceum. Some students and highway patrolmen were struck by gas canisters as the rabble-rousers moved back and forth, creating, at times, a solid mass of people, and at other times, pockets of participants huddled together leaving large swaths of grass clear. When the tear gas cleared, the mob surged once again toward the Lyceum only to be repelled by a volley of gas.

"The tear gas was so thick people were crying and puking and cursing," recalled Provost Ken Wooten, one of five student affairs directors on duty.[283] "The student affairs folks felt like we had an obligation to go out and try to get the students to go home. When we did, we were encircled."[284]

The second attack on Powledge occurred shortly after the first wave of tear gas engulfed The Circle. "I felt that the battle was going to be a long and that the hard core of the mob would not be satisfied with a little gas," Powledge said. He decided to stash his camera in Claude Sitton's car. Sitton had given him the car keys for that purpose. Turning on the radio to hear President Kennedy assure the nation that the campus was calm, rioters, having noticed Powledge's silhouette, surrounded the car. For Powledge it was terrifying: "I hunkered down side the car. There were people milling around, beating up anybody they didn't like. When it calmed down a bit, I sat up and vowed to myself I was going to get out of there."[285] A squad of marshals fired tear gas grenades over the top of the car, sending potential assailants running.[286]

Powledge, however, disputes Sitton's claim that the windshield was broken during the attack, admitting that, later, while covering the Newark riots, a car windshield was broken in another car he was driving.[287]

For reporters like Powledge, regional identity was not a factor in reporting the story, professionalism was: "The journalist's job, he said, "was to present the facts out there that you learned, heard from a speech, or saw with you own eyes and let the reader make his or her decision. You got to do that if you are going into were able to call yourself a journalist. You are always testing your own algorithm and a rioting situation is a place to test that."[288]

According to Powledge, the marshals maintained a straight line parallel to the front steps of the Lyceum and initially advanced only as far as the opposite side of the street. As the battle wore on, the marshals began entering the Circle, approaching the rioters in a wedge-shaped formation.

Powledge heard a state trooper complain about the tear gas, saying "something to the effect of, 'Those goddamn marshals. I wish I had some tear gas. I'd come back here and fix those bastards good.' The state police I saw seemed to be disgusted with the federal marshals because their own comfort had been invaded a bit."[289]

A third incident occurred when Powledge tried to leave the no-man's land between the mob and the marshals:

> If I got out of the car and walked or ran in the direction of the marshals, I would undoubtedly be mistaken for a rioter headed for them with some sort of destruction in mind. On the other hand, if I ran toward the rioters, I would be singled out as a newspaperman and would most probably [face] an even worse fate. So I decided to make it in the car which, after all, was rented.[290]

Observing the line of state police cars winding their way around the Circle, Powledge rolled down the window and asked first one, then another trooper if he could slip his car into the line of vehicles. The responses ranged from "No" to "Hell no." Powledge joined the line anyway, tagging along behind a Volkswagen also seeking an escape route. "I turned the car out in reverse as fast as I could, scraped the gears rather loudly, put it in drive and drove out behind the state policemen," he recalled.[291] "If anyone got in my way, I was just going to run them over. They got out of my way just as I set out in the white car."[292]

Powledge, who covered sit-ins in Atlanta and later other civil rights stories, started his journalism career in Connecticut with The Associated Press. When the Meredith story broke, he decided, "Because I was a Southerner, I—the thing that was happening there had been part of my life, was part of my life, obviously. And as a reporter it was something that I had to go investigate, had to go look into."[293] "The chief thing is that I was young, but also I was a southerner and knew there were a lot of southerners, some of them related to me, who were mean-assed people, they felt it was ok to hurt other people who didn't think like they do, still the same situation."[294] Powledge, who would go on to write for *The New York Times*, added:

U.S. Marshals surround Lyceum.
Photo by Ed Meek

115

We did not know how far the movement would go or where it would go or whether it would end or if so how it would end. We certainly didn't know what our role in it would be. I guess a lot of this was because for some strange reason most of us were younger then than we are now and—and we believed that we were immortal and therefore nothing bad could happen to us.[295]

AS MEREDITH ENROLLS
AT OLE MISS

- *Injury List Grows*
- *112 Arrested by U.S.*
The Atlanta Journal, Oct. 1, 1962

By Fred Powledge

Oxford, Miss., October 1 – James H. Meredith began attending classes at the University of Mississippi Monday as federal troops battled a mob of townspeople in the downtown area.

Federalized Mississippi troops fired at an angry mob in the streets of Oxford. Serious injuries were reported, although first details on this battle were sketchy.

Earlier, in the all-night riot on the campus, two persons were killed and at least 75 others wounded. Arrests by the US Justice Department were running over 100.

The latest announced figure of rounded-up rioters was 112, But others were being brought in. A spokesman for the Justice Department said about two thirds of them were outsiders.

By midmorning, federal troops had blocked highways into the town and were thoroughly searching all vehicles and people moving along with them.

Civilians leaving Oxford were told they would not be allowed to return without an emergency reason.

The downtown shooting occurred late Monday morning. Rioters began firing as troops of the 108 armored cavalry advanced down a street with drawn bayonets and rifles at the ready. The battle was about a half a block from the courthouse square.

Soldiers jumped from trucks and—on orders shouted by their officers—sprinted toward the rioters. The troops pushed the crowd steadily down the street.

Earlier, after the all-night campus fight, mobs of young men gathered about the square. They began throwing rocks and pop bottles at patrolling federal soldiers. At least one Army man was reported injured as the troops endured the barrage for about 15 minutes.

The soldiers closed ranks, put on their gas masks, advanced their rifles to the combat position and marched around the square. Some of the rioters retreated.

Teargas was fired at those who remained. It flowed across the square in gray clouds. Women shoppers staggered from stores, tears pouring down their faces. More troops poured in by the truckload.

Soon after the teargas was released, the mob began forming in back alleys to prepare another attack on the soldiers.

Overhead, a number of army helicopters hovered in the overcast sky, apparently ferrying troops from the airport to the battle area.

Other townspeople stood in groups at various intersections, shouting curses and throwing debris. One man waved a Confederate flag.

Many car windows were smashed, including the windshield of an Army transport truck. Business houses were closing their doors, evidently shutting down for the day. The rioters jeered the troops constantly in the meleé. They shouted:

"Yankee go home."

"Why don't you go to Cuba?"

"I'm a Nigger, why don't you come after me?"

United Press International reported that one state trooper, asked during the night rioting if he and his colleagues were going to move against the mob, said:

"You mean those bystanders?"

In Washington, Mississippi Representative Thomas G. Abernathy told the House "an inexperienced U.S. marshal" fired the first shot against a "group of kids who were doing nothing."

The formal business of registering Mr. Meredith was performed by registrar Robert Ellis, who did so under the threat of being held in contempt of court.

The Negro, who spent the night hidden from the mob and protected by a battery of marshals, thus became the first Negro to be knowingly registered as a student at the university.

The official act was a strange sight. The Confederate flag hung at half-staff before the building in which the registration occurred. Marshals surrounded the old Doric building.

Mr. Meredith marched out smiling and outwardly calm. His bodyguards got lost trying to locate his first class. It began to rain.

A crowd of students gathered. Impassioned and raging, they yelled:

"You got blood on your hands."

"Nigger, go home."

"How's it feel to have blood on your hands?"

An official of the Justice Department said marshals will escort Mr. Meredith around campus "as long as necessary. They won't leave him as long as he is in any danger."

Some 4,000 regular Army troops were in Oxford Monday morning, a spokesman said. This is almost as many people as live in the city: Oxford's population is 3283.

When Mr. Meredith appeared to be registered Monday morning, the campus was covered with litter and debris from the all night battle. The ground was strewn with expended tear gas shells, bricks, stones, broken soft drink bottles and about a half a dozen hulks of burned cars and trucks.

Two were killed. They were:

Paul Guihard, 30, New York based correspondent of the French news agency Agence France Presse. He was shot in the back and found dead on the campus.

Ray Gunter, 23, an Oxford jukebox repair man. He was dead on arrival at Oxford hospital.

The circumstances of both deaths remain a mystery.

Both men were shot with a 22 caliber revolver. Police said both bodies were found in approximately the same location.

They occurred as unit after unit of Army troops began rolling onto the embattled campus in a procession that continued all through the morning Monday. It was after 6 AM that an Army official was able to announce on the campus that "I now declare this area secure."

New fighting was to come later, however.

During most of the ear-lier time, the several hundred

Mississippi Highway Patrol men assigned to the campus stood by without doing a thing. University officials made no widespread attempt to put down the riot. The students met resistance only at the hands of the federal government when they tried to advance on the college administration building, which was surrounded by marshals wearing white helmet liners and carrying tear gas guns.

Meredith's Sunday entrance on the campus came as a surprise for most people here, who had expected the Federal government to make its attempt on Monday. Observers felt the earlier time was chosen for two reasons:

1. To get the Negro on the campus unexpectedly.

2. To give Gov. Ross Barnett an opportunity to comply with federal court orders rather than to try to arrest him on contempt charges.

A federal government build-up of men and materials started early Sunday morning, when an engineer group arrived at nearby Holly Springs National Forest and started constructing a "tent city" in a grown-up pasture. This was to house the task force of marshals.

But the marshals came in mid-afternoon to Oxford airport instead. They were equipped with weapons and helmets and herded into Army two and a half-ton trucks. The trucks started downtown. Most observers expected the trucks to continue out to the national forest. But as they approached the gate of the university, the trucks turned in.

The marshals surrounded the administration building, and federal officials went inside. Newsmen were excluded from the campus at this point.

Later, about 6:15 CDT (4:15 EST), Mr. Meredith arrived by airplane. He went to the campus in a private car preceded and followed by two trucks full of marshals. Very few people noted this arrival.

It was about 7:30 PM when the students, and others, some of whom came in cars from Alabama and Louisiana, started their protest against the federal government and James Meredith.

The US marshals stood firm for half an hour, but then, when students started throwing bottles and bricks at the marshals, and shouting obscene words at them, a flying squad of federal man ran after the students.

119

The marshals fired teargas guns. The students fled.

But they came back, many times, to face the teargas.

Late in the battle, former US Army Gen. Edwin A. Walker appeared on the campus to lead a charge on the administration building, Mr. Walker jumped on a Confederate Memorial and said:

"If you can't win, go home. Don't stay at the University, but, let's not quit. We can win."

Students commandeered a fire truck and tried to turn hoses on the marshals; bottles and bricks were thrown at the officers, and several students tried to smash into the building with a bulldozer.

The students did not know this, but the 200 marshals at this time, some three hours after the riots started, were running dangerously low on tear gas shells, their primary weapons.

At what must've been nearly the last moment, a convoy of jeeps and personnel carriers bearing National Guardsmen in green fatigues, with gas masks and rifles, rode up the long street which connects the university with the town of Oxford.

Many of the remaining 1,000 students and others who were rioting at this point decided then to go home. But some stayed to shout obscenities and throw bricks at the guardsmen.

Early Monday morning, additional troops from the federalized Mississippi National Guard and some regular Army men were dispatched to the campus. Included in the fresh troops were an 1,100-man infantry battle group and a group of combat-trained military police.

Through it all, Mr. Meredith remained on the University of Mississippi campus. This reporter, who was caught between the students and the marshals in an automobile, saw students attempt on numerous occasions to sneak up on the marshals and throw things at them. But each time the students were picked out by flashlights or searchlights and then forced back by tear gas.

A little earlier, when the press, radio and television were allowed on campus, the students decided to vent their wrath on reporters and photographers.

Gordon Yoder, a film a cameraman for Telenews, Dallas, Texas, was the first to feel the anger of the mob.

As Mr. Yoder and his wife approached the administration building in their automobile, students stopped it, broke its windows, flattened its fenders, took Mr. Yoder's camera away from him and smashed it.

Two Mississippi state patrolmen asked the students to "move back" but the students refused. The Yoders were finally removed by police car. Their automobile was a total loss.

The incident was repeated on a minor scale many more times. This writer was struck by a student because he was from Atlanta. Others had their cameras taken away and broken.

The students made numerous charges on Army vehicles parked in front of the administration building. They let air from the trucks tires, shot a fire extinguisher into a cab, and set a canvas roof on fire.

When later contingents of marshals arrived, the students threw cigarettes and curses at them.

A Decatur man with a 7.7 German Mauser rifle was arrested in the Oxford rioting. Authorities were attempting to determine if he was the sniper who had been operating from one of the campus buildings upper floor and taking pot shots at marshals and federalized Mississippi national guardsmen.

The arrested man was identified as Melvin Bruce, a mechanic, of 2937 Westbury Dr., Decatur. He was brought in handcuffs into military headquarters at the university, where he joined a more than 25 other prisoners. The slightly built man was wearing a navy pea jacket and dungarees.

GORDON YODER

The first serious attack on newsmen occurred at 7 p.m. when Telenews videographer Gordon Yoder and his wife Irene's red and white Chrysler Town Car station wagon entered The Circle. Students stopped the car, pounded on the hood and screamed for the occupants to get out.

Emerging from the vehicle and clutching his lights and camera, Yoder was swarmed by the mob. He had been pelted by rocks in Pine Bluff, Arkansas, on a 1959 school integration assignment, and worked as a military photographer during World War II and the Korean War.[296] He had never lost a camera, including his first one, a still-camera he received at age eight, the same year he won first prize in a photography contest. He was not about to lose his equipment to hoodlums in Mississippi.[297] His experience at Ole Miss "was a real sticky situation," he told Department of Justice investigators. "The worse thing I have ever been in."[298]

Gene Sherman of *The Los Angeles Times* put Yoder's experience into perspective in his dispatch from Oxford describing mob violence: "as a terrible, paralyzing thing to witness... You can feel it congeal and fester, and spread, and then a helpless sorrow grips your heart. It builds slowly but erupts quickly.[299] For Yoder, it was his reality as he sought to protect himself, his wife, his equipment and his car. He had been professional photographer for 25 years, starting his career with Jamieson Film in Dallas in 1937 and moving up to shooting newsreels for Paramount News in 1943.[300] That experience was for naught in Oxford. Sherman wrote:

> They grabbed [Yoder's] camera and smashed it, The couple took refuge in their station wagon, but yelling students encircled it, and they were unable to move it. The sound welled up, interspersed with the tinkle of broken glass; students began beating on the car and kicking dents into the door and fenders.[301]

The state troopers, having orders to prevent newsmen from entering the campus until Meredith arrived, refused to come to the Yoders' aid until the mob turned on Irene and dragged her out of the car by her hair. The troopers helped the couple to safety, but not before Yoder's film equipment was smashed.[302]

The Yoders were not the only broadcasters targeted. The bulky TV equipment was a dead giveaway. All evening, there were reports of rioters ordering cameramen to surrender their cameras or face physical violence.

Mrs. Yoder had driven her husband to campus, planning to drop him off, and then park the car.[303] Yoder wanted to film the marshals stationed in front of the Lyceum while there was enough daylight. He recalled:

> I got out of the car because there were some students whose other cars were in the way. I started to walk up through the crowd of students right in the street towards the marshals. I

saw/suspected nothing at the time that could cause any trouble for me. A state police car had just gone through the crowd and opened up a path and I walked straight up this path through the students, ringed with students on both sides.[304]

At this point a trooper detained Yoder: "I was trying to explain to him that they had to let us in, and he said no. And I said, 'Well why don't you call your superior so we can get over here and find this out... I am entitled to be here. I'm doing my job.'" Before the trooper could verify this information the students attacked the Yoders' car, kicking in the doors, before assaulting the couple.[305]

G. Michael Lala, a cameraman with WDSU-TV in New Orleans, recalled that he heard someone yell, "There's a newsman!" Another man said, "Get a rope! Get a rope!"[306] Yoder said students started pulling at his bulky broadcast camera: "I held onto it very firmly and this was the first time I got any physical violation of my body—I was hit in the back. It felt like a fellow raised his knees and hit me in the back."[307]

As Yoder struggled to save his equipment, two troopers pushed him toward the crowd, then changed their minds and pulled him out. It was a scene reminiscent of the Keystone Cops, minus the comedy. Two more troopers joined the pair, and together they hustled Yoder through the mob:

> [They] just threw me to the dogs, so to speak, because, by this time, the crowd was ready to run around and come after me. I had not made one print (shot) of film; I did not turn on my light one time; I did not shoot one picture. I had my camera. Never raised my camera to my eye to shoot. I never turned on the light. [308]

Yoder begged the troopers to take him to his Chrysler. Two responded and escorted him to the car. He slid into the back seat and locked the doors.

But his ordeal was not over. A state trooper car pulled in front of the station wagon, blocking their escape. Yoder recalled:

My wife could have driven out if the troopers had let her, but they said, "No, no, back out." And, if she'd slammed the horn down and put her foot on the gas, we'd have gotten out of there because those kids just won't stand in front of a big, heavy, moving car, and they'd never stood a chance to turn it over; but the trooper said, "No, no, back out." By that time, we were ringed in by the kids. They really came and poured around us. [309]

More than 15 vehicles were burned the night of September 30. Photo by Ed Meek

Although the doors were locked, the driver's window was rolled down, enabling a student to lunge past Irene Yoder and reach for the camera. "One big idiot stuck his whole body and kept screaming 'Give me the camera, give me the camera,' And I said 'I haven't shot any pictures. I'm not going to give you the camera. Get out of the car.'"[310] Mrs. Yoder called it "a complete madhouse."[311]

The attacker screamed "nigger-lovin' Yankee bitch" at Mrs. Yoder, a native of Jackson, Mississippi. A coed asked a companion, "Lord, Joe, what are they gonna do to that woman?"

"Kill her, I guess," the boy replied. "She's a nigger-lover, isn't she?" [312]

Yoder remembered saying, "Officer, officer, get this hoodlum out of here. I didn't call him a bum... I called him hoodlum."[313] A trooper kept telling this boy "Come on, come on, get out of the car, come on, get out, get, out," but made no effort to make him get out. And he's a big devil; he was big, and screaming and furious right in our face.[314]

Finally, the trooper pulled the boy out of the window. Meanwhile, the mob kicked in the headlights, broke the radio antenna, smashed the windshield, kicked the doors and started rocking the car. The idea was to overturn the car with its occupants inside. *Newsday* reporter Michael Dorman said he saw a state trooper assisting the mob in attempting to overturn the station wagon.[315]

At this point, other troopers assisted the couple into a patrol car. In the process, the bulky TV camera Yoder had clung to throughout the attack was snatched from his arms. The Yoders left behind another camera, a brief case, a tripod, a case with lenses and several loose lenses. Mrs. Yoder lost a shoe. Yoder was bruised and had a sore jaw from a rioter's headlock. Troopers drove the station wagon off campus accompanied by state police vehicles with emergency lights shining and sirens wailing. It was later found vandalized with items removed from the glove compartment.

Harold Kluehe, a NBC staff soundman who recorded the encounter along with his cameraman, said a student in the area approached him and asked if he was a newsman. Kluehe replied that he was with NBC. The youth said, "If you value your life, I advise you to get out of here with your equipment. They've gone crazy here."[316]

UNIVERSITY OF MISSISSIPPI INTEGRATION RIOT

Universal-International News (text)

Filmed by Gordon Yoder
October 1, 1962

James H. Meredith is formally enrolled at the University of Mississippi, ending one chapter in the federal government's efforts to desegregate the university. The town of Oxford is an armed camp following riots that accompanied the registration of the first Negro in the university's 118 year history. Much of this film record was destroyed when our cameraman, Gordon Yoder, was attacked, but he did salvage pictures of Gov. Ross Barnett at the scene. The governor fought the court order long and bitterly before modifying his stand, saying Mississippi was overpowered by the federal government.

President Kennedy appealed to the students and to the people of the state to comply peacefully with the law and bring the crisis to an end. Even as he talked, riots were breaking out in Oxford: "Americans are free, in short, to disagree with the law but not to disobey it. For in a government of laws and not of men, no man, however prominent or powerful, and no mob, however unruly or boisterous, is entitled to defy a court of law. If this country should ever reach the point where any man or group of men by force or threat of force could long deny the commands of our court and our Constitution, then no law would stand free from doubt, no judge would be sure of his writ, and no citizen would be safe from his neighbors."

Nearly six thousand troops patrol Oxford to maintain order; and arrests mount to more than 200, as smaller disturbances erupt the next day. Former Major General Edwin Walker, who came here from his home in Texas, is put under arrest and held on high bail on charges of inciting insurrection. He was flown to a federal prison hospital as relative calm settled on the town in the greatest crisis the South has faced since the civil war.

RICHARD VALERIANI

As events unfolded NBC reporter Richard Valeriani had to switch from recording film stories for television to producing audio reports for radio, a dual task many broadcast reporters found themselves in during the early days of televsion news. That meant that, on the night of September 30, Valeriani had to dash to campus to update his film material and then scamper back to his motel to phone in his radio stories for the hourly news shows.

It took time and energy to do both. Valeriani relied on stringers to fill in the gaps.

The stringers were a diverse trio: "Doc" Duncan Whiteside, campus adviser for radio station WCBH; Ole Miss student "Skip" Schultz; and Bill Silver, whose father, history professor James Silver, lived on campus and was a Meredith supporter. Bill Silver said the rioters targeted the press because "they felt we were helping Meredith's cause and the cause of integration. As they used to say, we were outside agitators, when, in reality, they were the agitators."[317]

Television cameras weighed about 20 pounds—videotape with its lighter cameras was not yet in use—and were tethered to a

Student demonstrators arrested and detained in the Lyceum. Photo by Ed Meek

soundman with illumination provided by a light man. "The danger was not the weight [of the camera]. They had a metal piece that went around their waist and up to the camera. The lights were [what was] dangerous at night," Valeriani recalled.[318] The lights made the broadcasters a target.

Valerian recalled, "There was shooting. There was tear gas. There were stones thrown. I remember it was as scary as hell.[319] Valeriani, who served as the Midwestern correspondent for NBC, said he "was new to violent situations. As a reporter, I am the outsider. I am like the village idiot. I can go in and think no one is going to harm me. You are just observing. I found out later that the people storming the Lyceum thought they were going to do harm.[320]

During the evening, Whiteside and Schultz took up positions in the Fine Arts building overlooking the Circle and recorded their descriptions. Silver roamed the campus and served as a guide for the NBC team.[321]

Valeriani said that his biggest challenge was getting a long-distance connection to file his stories. "I was pleased with myself for getting the story out every hour. It is no good to have a story if you can't get it on the air."[322] With over 300 reporters present in Oxford, the competition for the 29 long distance lines was fierce.

"What I had tried to do was to find a phone in some little place on the second floor, get my notes and come back and do a radio report. You had to dial at least 100 times to get a line out," he said.[323] It was not unusual for a reporter, once he had finished his call, to pass a telephone with an open line to another reporter. Operators would then transfer the call to the second reporter's office.

Such cooperation, while not widely discussed, was not uncommon. In Oxford, William Gordon, a staff correspondent for the *Newark (N.J.) Evening News,* explained, "The activity on campus on September 30, 1962, and October 1, 1962, was so widespread that it was impossible for one person to personally witness all of the developments." [324] Gordon added reporters frequently gathered at their hotels to exchange information and, it would appear, to check up on the safety and well-being of their colleagues.

Journalists are competitive when it comes to the story, but they are a band of brothers. If one newsman is injured, the threat exists for all. It is for that reason that the murder of Paul Guihard still resonates among the reporters who were at Ole Miss in 1962. "It was so chaotic and the reporters who covered that sort of thing—they tended to know each other in a pack way—the same reporters turned up at the same stories so they tended not to make friends with outsiders," Valeriani recalled.[325]

Valeriani believes that the presence of the cameras at Ole Miss and at other venues during the civil rights movement contributed to "the improvement of the quality of the coverage by other media."

> It forced a lot of people to get out of their offices and off the phones out into the street to watch what was happening; and it made it a lot more difficult for those newspapers who put those pictures back in the drawer or back in the morgue or didn't carry the story, because they saw it on television and their readers wanted to know where it was in their newspapers.[326]

In Mississippi, this was easier said than done. Valeriani found that the NBC affiliate in Jackson was run by a member of the Citizens Council after WLBT-TV station technicians refused to air his reports.

Because of licensing agreements, the station eventually complied, but ran a disclaimer regarding content. "I'd come up and do a story, and the station would come on and say, 'This station has no responsibility whatsoever for that fake and phony report you just saw—or something like that.'"[327]

For Valeriani, who grew up in Bridgeton, New Jersey, and graduated from Yale University, heading south to cover the civil rights movement was outside his experience:

> I grew up in southern New Jersey. We say our only race problem was that we didn't know we had a problem. But, I went to integrated schools, I went to parties and social events with black people—Negroes, as they were called, and colored people. And so when I got to the South and saw this, frankly, I was shocked. I mean, really shocked. There were a lot of people [who] had mentioned the separate lunch counters and drinking fountains and restrooms. So, it was shocking because somewhere in the back of my mind, I'd seen movies or read about it, but to go there and see it. And then, be exposed to the ferocity and bias and prejudice was really a shock.[328]

He added. "The standard answer, however, to the question of how much of a role did the camera play in shaping events is, there were no cameras at the Boston Tea Party."[329]

Valeriani later was nearly killed when he was hit with an ax handle wielded by a man who had warned him not to cover a 1965 demonstration in Marion, Alabama. He observed, "I think that obviously the movement leaders decided to go to Birmingham because Bull Connor was there; and they decided to go to Selma because Jim Clark was there. And they knew how Bull Connor would react, and they knew how Jim Clark would react, and they knew how that would affect the rest of the nation."[330] Valeriani was also a journalist of the traditional school, one who adhered to the strictest objectivity:

> I knew the difference between right and wrong, but my job was to put the story on the air. As the cliché goes in our business, "When both sides are complaining, you think you're doing a good job." You've heard about how the white power

structure—agitators stirring up all the trouble. They complained about that. The people in the movement complained that I wasn't helping them enough. I was trying to explain that that was not my job.[331]

I have to tell you that I did not consider myself as a sympathetic referee at the time. I really did consider myself a reporter; I tried to be a reporter. And I thought of myself as something of a schizophrenic that I had one set of feelings on the job; I had no question as to what was right and what was wrong on this issue, but that I was not there to write editorials. I was there to report. There were two sides of the story, and I was only doing my job if I reported both sides of the story. Frequently I used to get complaints from both sides, and I felt then that I was doing my job right. [332]

Valeriani, who went off to cover most of the civil rights demonstrations across the South, concluded, "For starters, when I was covering Oxford and Selma and Philadelphia and Birmingham, I was not aware that I was covering a seminal period in American history. I was doing it story by story. I was covering the trees at the time. I didn't see the forest, which came much later."[333]

James Meredith arriving in the Lyceum to register for his first class.
Photo by Ed Meek

By the end of the 1960s he would observe, "I thought those of us who did that were part of the coming of age of television news. We became, for the first time, really respected across the land. And, as I say, it had tremendous impact."[334]

"NBC SPECIAL REPORT FROM MISSISSIPPI"

NBC RADIO NEWS ON THE HOUR (October 1, 1962)

Reported by Richard Valeriani

This was the scene on the campus of Ole Miss last night. The lights of cars bearing federal marshals were moved to the campus from a naval air station outside Memphis. The first arrivals on the campus was greeted without incident, there was no trouble. But then when word spread that Negro Air Force veteran James Meredith was on the campus and had been brought to Ole Miss to register, the fighting started.

The battle became more deadly. Snipers opened fire on the marshals, several were wounded. Federalized guardsmen from Oxford were rushed to the battle scene, followed by regular Army troops from their standby in Memphis.

One after midnight the military forces drove the rioters off campus, the rioting swept downtown. More troops arrived and were bombarded with flying objects along the streets. Several were hit, windshields were smashed.

By early morning, the battle was over. Two men were dead, almost 200 injured. In the grey morning light, flames still flickered among the charred hulks of cars burned by the rioters. The acrid smell of tear gas hung thickly in the air. The Lyceum area was littered with rocks and broken glass and hundreds of spent tear gas canisters.

DOROTHY BUTLER GILLIAM

Washington Post reporter Dorothy Butler Gilliam was not in Mississippi the night of September 30. "Can you imagine a black woman being on campus as a reporter covering the events of September 30-October 1? The *Washington Post* sent a white reporter to cover the events on campus," she said. Gilliam arrived a week after the crisis began.[335]

Gilliam later observed, "Just the act of covering the (Meredith) story—to me, as a black reporter—felt very much what it might feel like to any reporter in a war zone because there really was that kind of constant level of fear."[336]

Gilliam had been working for the *Post* for almost a year and was one of three black reporters on the staff. Being hired at a metropolitan daily, she said, was very rare for a black woman: "During this time, the daily press was just extraordinarily segregated. In fact, they had only begun to write about blacks in the mid-fifties, around the time of the school segregation and the school desegregation cases."[337]

When it came time to assign reporters to Oxford, *Post* editors sent white reporter Bill Chapman, even though Gilliam wanted to cover the story despite the danger.[338] "Mississippi is a place that just evokes all kinds of fear and feelings in any sane black person. I certainly had my share of worry and concern about going to Mississippi," she said. "Mississippi was watching its most cherished notions being challenged, so it was just rising up in fury."[339]

This was not her first assignment covering school integration. Reporting on the integration of Little Rock Central High School had prepared Gilliam for Meredith and Ole Miss. It was in Little Rock that outraged white citizens blocked the admission of nine students because of the color of their skin. Television hit the national airwaves with images of screaming women, their faces distorted, shocking the nation. President Dwight D. Eisenhower sent in federal troops to quell the disturbance, the first in what would become a series of school integration battles played out in the media.

Disregarding orders from Memphis *Tri-State Defender* Editor Alex Wilson to stay in Tennessee, Gilliam headed to Little Rock with photographer Ernest Withers. She wanted to be part of the reporting team. To Gilliam, the Little Rock story was about law and order and the rights of citizens to receive an education: "The story was, this is what it took to really enforce the law of the land. This is how deeply entrenched the anti-black feelings were. This is how strongly the white people felt about their rights to an education that totally excluded blacks. So the story was that *Brown v. Board of Education* had been probably the most important racial story in terms of how we started opening a new America."[340]

In Little Rock, Gilliam saw firsthand how civil rights leaders, activists and reporters swapped information and shared strategies and perspectives: "I don't think because you were there being a part of the story meant that you weren't being a journalist. I think what I was doing, I was using my special access to enrich and enliven the story... We know that reporters and government officials and reporters and sources have often talked and traded information, so I have no discomfort with that."[341] Being part of the chaos and writing copy on the fly was energizing to her as a young reporter and prepared her for similar assignments.

As frightening as Little Rock was, Gilliam said it did not compare to the fear she felt in Mississippi in 1962. "This was a tough and frightening assignment, especially in view of the fury that had already killed the French journalist. Black life was cheap in Mississippi."[342]

Jazz singer Effie Burt, a black woman who as a child lived in Oxford in 1962, could attest to such worries. Burt said the fear was so real that in the days and weeks after the riots her family purchased groceries out of town and avoided public situations to protect themselves from violence.[343] Burt, who was nine years old in 1962, recalled stories passed down through the generations about the infamous "lynching tree" located on the east side of the courthouse. The family prepared for the worst as news of the riot at Ole Miss spread through their community.

Her father, Leonard Burt, owner of a 130-acre farm outside Oxford, was active in civil rights activities. During the integration crisis, he met with his white contacts and used the information to keep his family and friends informed of developments, telling them when it was safe, or not, to go into town.[344]

It was in this backdrop, after a week of turmoil in Oxford that Editor Ben Gilbert sent Gilliam to Oxford. She had been at the *Post* for just about a year, after earning a master's degree from Columbia University:

> As you know, the South was a dangerous violent place when it came to blacks. Blacks were kept as second-, third-, fourth-, fifth-class citizens and with threats of violence, it was a horrible way of life. But Mississippi, even in that hostile climate, was a case apart and Mississippi—one person once called it the evil wonder of the world. And it had open violence... and the Ku Klux Klan just dominated. Its whole job was to keep black people in their place. Segregation was written into the laws, meaning the Democratic Party bylaws, it was enforced by lawmakers, the police force, the

sheriffs, the White Citizens Council. Everything that you could imagine worked against blacks ever achieving equality. And the blacks who lived there just were trapped, many of them in almost the same kind of lifestyle they had in slavery.[345]

Such reservations, however, didn't stop her from heading to the Magnolia State. Gilliam asked Withers to accompany her to Oxford, because Withers not only knew the South, but "he knew how to negotiate, which meant doing whatever he had to do; if he had to say "yes" or "no sir"—you know, bow to these old nasty, bigoted, racist whites, he would do it. He would get us out of there."[346]

Withers' abilities proved useful during the 70-mile trip between Memphis and Oxford when "sheriffs or vigilantes with gun racks on top of their cars" stopped their car."[347] Gilliam recalled: "He (Withers) had Tennessee tags on his car, of course, and we were just stopped by, you know, these whites, who were 'just checking tags,' you know. 'All right, what are you doing here, niggers?' And he would get out, and he'd talk to these people with guns, and yes I was afraid, there was no doubt about it."[348]

Withers, who had trained as a policeman, knew the wisdom of saying little in a tense situation. "I mean I had fear, but I had a sense of self-confidence and a tactic that you always have in life, that you know how to act anywhere you go, to keep yourself, if you can keep your head on, all about you. It's the same philosophy that makes one act and live safely; so I had no problem."[349]

Gilliam's assignment in Oxford was to report on reactions in the black community to the integration crisis and to interview black leaders. "I could get people to talk to me who might not have talked so openly with a white reporter," she said, noting that she could obtain information from the black community that a white reporter could not.[350] Gilliam interviewed Meredith's wife and NAACP field secretary Medgar Evers during the week she was in Mississippi.

> We got into Oxford and you know, the whole place seemed to be in flames... But anyway, the culture was to kill a black person if they made a misstep, that's the whole, that's the bottom line about Mississippi. So there was great fear in the black community

because here were the troops, all these reporters, and they knew that kind of once all that was over, they felt like they were going to be left with these white people who would, who would do anything to them.[351]

Arriving in Oxford, Gilliam found white reporters were loath to share information, much less information like the location of pay telephones or tips about pending news conferences. Restaurants were segregated, as were other public facilities.

Housing was scarce in Oxford because of the influx of reporters and, for black reporters, even scarcer. The travel office at the *Post* arranged for housing for its white reporters traveling in the South, but Gilliam was on her own when faced with a scarcity of segregated facilities.[352] Withers secured a quiet spot for Gilliam the first night—at a black funeral home.[353]

> The first night at the funeral home, if tear gas was being felt over there on the campus of Ole Miss, tears were probably flowing from my eyes by about 3 a.m. because there was this colossal noise and I thought "What is going on?" You do not want to hear lots of noise in a funeral home in the middle of the night in Oxford, Mississippi, not in 1962. So it turned out that a couple of black men had been killed during the night and they were being brought directly to the funeral home. And Withers told me there was nothing to worry about; you're going to be just fine.[354]

Gilliam recalled that she looked in the local newspaper the next day for a story about the murders and found none, a fact that did not surprise her, because "that was a way almost of instilling fear in the local people."[355] Years later, a university official challenged Gilliam's story, saying, "I don't remember any death being reported in the black community during that fracas." Gilliam replied, "If you think about all the deaths that go unreported in black communities, I know that it doesn't seem likely in the sense that you would think that the press would be all over it, and I don't know if they chose not to make a big deal of it, [or] if the community, in its fear, chose not to make a big deal of it."[356]

In their book, *The Race Beat,* Gene Roberts and Hank Klibanoff, noted: "For the most part, [newspapers] treated Negro communities as a creepy corner of the world not worthy of their readers' time. Many newspapers didn't carry any news at all about Negroes; some printed only social snippets under such headlines as 'Activities of Colored People.' And some devoted a full page to Negro news in editions circulated only in Negro neighborhoods... The papers didn't carry Negro wedding announcements or obituaries."[357]

There were few black reporters on the civil rights beat. Most worked for small, underfunded black newspapers, often weeklies, or for black magazines such as *Jet* and *Ebony.* But Gilliam noted: "It was the black press that really helped to push the Civil Rights movement. Had it not been for a very active black press working from approximately 1910 to 1950, I think the civil rights movement would have had a much slower start."[358] Gilliam was part of that push starting her career at the *Louisville Defender* at age 17, taking over the society pages when the society editor became ill. She was in her first year of college. Black papers were not viewed as competitors by the large national daily newspapers and magazines because of their much smaller circulations. Black reporters also had to contend with racial discrimination in terms of transportation, housing and dining. On the job, they had better access to the black community but access to power brokers, segregationists and law enforcement was often restricted.

Gilliam recalled that, in 1962, there were only three blacks on the *Post* staff. [359] The American Newspaper Guild reported 45 black reporters employed at predominately white newspapers in 1964 during a time when there were about 50,000 people working in newspaper editorial positions.[360] *New York Times* editor Turner Catledge summed up the problem, noting: "Finding a qualified Negro reporter on those days was almost impossible."[361] He did not address the extent of recruitment efforts. But it would seem logical that major newspapers would seek out black reporters to provide access, which white reporters weren't able to secure, but there also was concern that black reporters might be biased if assigned to civil rights stories. The

Kerner Commission in 1968 called the hiring of more African-American reporters imperative.[362]

Gilliam's path to journalism was unlikely. The daughter of an African Methodist Episcopal minister, Gilliam was born in Memphis, a segregated city, and moved as a child to northern Kentucky, where she attended segregated schools. "I was used to the hand-me-down books. I think I wasn't aware of all this because we lived in black neighborhoods and we were, we certainly had a very full life."[363] However, she recalled that the message she received in her community was that "we were capable and we were equal... I became a reporter, not because I had role models, because I don't remember seeing—there were no black people on the television... There were no black reporters on the news (or at) the daily newspaper in my hometown... Journalism really opened doors to worlds that an individual never would have an opportunity to see open, certainly in the way that journalism does."[364]

James Meredith and his parents,
Moses "Cap" Meredith and Roxie Patterson Meredith
Photo by Wofford Smith.

MISSISSIPPI MOOD: HOPE AND FEAR

The Washington Post "Outlook," Sunday, Oct. 14, 1962

by Dorothy Gilliam

Oxford, Miss. Hope and fear are the moods of Negroes in Mississippi these anxious days.

You can spot these feelings in the hesitant words of a disenfranchised Negro handyman in Oxford who hobbles heavily to a chair, hikes up his overalls, and talks.

Or in the bold words of a harassed Negro leader who, despite constant danger, declares that James H. Meredith's entry into the University of Mississippi "is a clear breakthrough" for Negroes and will be a springboard for other advances.

The hope is that Meredith signals the coming of the light for all of them. The fear is that the inevitable changes will bring further death, destruction and repercussions.

These are impressions from a swing through Mississippi last week. People talked freely because they were talking to another Negro. The major apprehension is about what will occur when the wrath of white Mississippians is no longer throttled by the federal presence.

"Anything can happen," the Mississippi born handyman declared darkly.

An Oxford-born woman who works in the tiny town's only Negro boardinghouse, said she was saving her money so she could leave with the troops. "I'm going to Ioway," is the way she put it. "I don't feel safe here with the soldiers out. But I still hope a lot more colored kids get in that school."

Behind these fears is the pride, the hope, and the distant vision of change that exhilarates and scares them at the same time. Their feelings are similar to those of Negroes all over the state in the wake of Meredith's desegregation of Ole Miss.

The extent of each of these moods depends on whether you live in Jackson or in the vast Delta; on whether you're a lawyer or a plowboy or a man who loses his job because of James H Meredith.

In Oxford, a 29-year-old man who moved there from Chicago last February lost his $6-a-day job in the grill at Ole Miss last week. "The younger busboys heard 'nigger' once too often. They walked off. I had to go, too. But the boss came after me later that night, and I went back. Then he fired me. I was glad. It was a rather small contribution. When a white man first called me 'boy' down here, it was like a slap in the face. Then you get used to it. When the odds are this much against you, you get to the place where you don't hurt no more."

Like Gov. Ross R. Barnett, many Negroes had said "never" to desegregation in their lifetimes. But in their heads, not in their hearts.

Why? Why did they believe, like the whites, that Barnett could buck the whole might and majesty of the federal government?

Negroes familiar with the state's history and politics explain that Mississippi's devotion to white supremacy and segregation is kept alive by politicians, ministers and big business. Until blood flowed on the streets of Oxford, there was no break in this pattern.

"All these elements," said Memphis attorney A. W. Willis, "have cooperated since the Civil War to advance black inferiority and separation. Those who didn't like it, he continued, got out if they could; the others acquiesced.

"Mississippi," offered Russell B. Sugarman, another Memphis attorney, is now a controlled state."

The success of the technique is reflected both in Negroes' incredulity and in the frank admission by one of Oxford's few Negro businessmen. "One of our greatest handicaps here is getting over that inferior feeling."

Ironically, a slim Negro student in Jackson suggested that *Ebony* magazine editor Lerone Bennett's recent description of southern Negroes at the turn-of-the-century captures many of Mississippi's present day frustrations.

Bennett wrote:

". . . to be powerless and to curse one's self for cowardice, to be conditioned by dirt and fear and shame and signs, to become a part of the signs and to feel them in the deepest recesses of the spirit . . .to be a plaything of judges and courts and policemen, to be black in a white fire and to believe. Finally in one's own unworthiness, to be without books and words and pretty pictures . . . without the rationalizations of psychology and sociology . . . to give in finally, to bow, to scrape, to grin, and to hate oneself for one's servility and weakness and blackness . . ."

Yet the element of hope springs up almost miraculously and in the most unexpected people and places.

Roger Thompson, 63, a retired carpenter at Ole Miss, laid aside his saw and stepped gingerly off the splintery porch he was repairing to talk to a reporter. "I am so glad there's a black face over there," he said in a kind of a squeal with a flinging of his arm toward the campus. "I'm proud of it and I hope there'll be more. I'm not afraid. And you can use my name!"

An Oxford businessman who didn't want his name used said change was on its way, led by men like Meredith and by young Negroes he hoped would return to the state. "We have that inward feeling that progress is being made, but we don't talk about it much around here," he said.

In Mississippi, the saying is reversed, talk is expensive.

Medger Evers, NAACP field secretary, thinks Meredith's move will ignite voter registration again and spur other educational gains all over the state. Petitions are pending to desegregate local schools in Jackson and Leake county, he said.

"And we are going to make it known to high school and college students that Meredith's suit was designed to break down barriers in all institutions of higher learning," he said. "But we don't expect to win without a fight."

A home economics teacher at Oxford's only Negro high school said several students told her they were going to study real hard so they, too, could go to Ole Miss.

While Meredith is no knight in shining armor, he appears to be pretty close to it to people too long without hope. Yet some Negroes refuse to lift him onto a pedestal because they believe it gives the impression that he is a freak, a Mississippi accident, as it were.

"Meredith," said Sugarman, the Memphis lawyer, "is just a Mississippi boy who went home."

But fear follows closely on the heels of hope. Fear of

physical violence, of economic repercussion, of change itself, Negroes say.

Some soft-pedal this. Like the youngish businessman in Jackson who said Mississippi is hell for Negroes, but stoutly insisted that the Negro is more fearless these days and won't stand for any white folks' guff or be scared off.

But he was afraid to give his name.

Medger Evers thinks there is fear. "I don't know to what degree, but it greater in the rural areas where you cannot count on local police protection."

During our interview, Evers phone rang. The caller reported that eight Negro homes had been strafed by shotguns allegedly held by youthful whites.

Evers immediately called the Justice Department in Washington and asked for federal protection for the families. There was not any need to bother with the local officials, he declared.

Jackson's Dr. Albert B. Britton, a member of the Civil Rights Committee, thinks the fear on both sides is a fear of change. But he thinks the moderates can quiet the rabble—if enough of them speak out.

Oxford's only Negro funeral director, G.W. Bankhead, doesn't put much stock in a flare up of violence. "If it comes it'll come from only the sorriest folks. And we've got enough law and order here to take care of it."

In the wake of the bloody riots, NAACP state president Aaron Henry, a Clarksdale pharmacist, wired President Kennedy to declare martial law and fan marshals over the state to act as registrars for six months.

"With the Negro vote," said Henry, "will come a liberation to Mississippi of thousands of both white and Negro citizens who are now caught up in the web of static politics."

"Yet," said R. Jess Brown, a Jackson lawyer, "there's a little ray of light" from white moderates. He referred to an editorial in the *Jackson Times* last Thursday. "Was it not inevitable that Federal bayonets would lay a shadow across the heart of Mississippi? Anyone—working man or banker—should know that when he walks into a court of law of the United States of America he is walking into an atmosphere of congealed experience that has fashioned the strongest government and the finest nation that man has ever placed on the map. It revolves around one word—freedom.

145

"Mississippians have found the 'Law' hard to stomach within the past two weeks.

"But the menu was inevitable, citizens. It did become abundantly clear since the Supreme Court decision of 1954 and even further back—the ratification of Section 1 of the 14th amendment in 1868 that the dish was on its way. It was piping hot, and tinged with ingredients that sting the pallet . . ."

In addition to the obvious fears, there is the psychological warfare, as it were, the subtle repercussions.

A home economics teacher at Oxford's only Negro high school said two whites trailed her as she drove from Oxford to Batesville, their headlights glaring down her neck. She said she didn't know what to expect. Finally they pulled out, shouted absurdities and sped past.

Notably missing is the humor among Negroes about the present state of affairs. The southern white press was having a field day with Bobby and the rest of the Kennedys.

The Oxford businessman who couldn't give his name explained it this way: "At this point we are too concerned to find much that is funny."

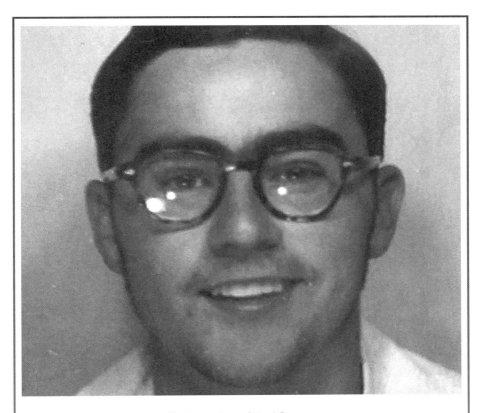

NEAL GREGORY

Oxford is a church-going town. Methodist, Episcopal, Baptist, Presbyterian and Roman Catholic churches are within a stone's throw of each other. The competition for parking spaces is tough on Sunday morning. On October 7, after a week of turmoil in Oxford, Neal Gregory of *The Memphis Commercial Appeal* set out to capture the mood of the residents. To do so, he visited the churches.

A common message came from the pulpits, a plea for tolerance and repentance. The Rev. Duncan Gray Jr., of St. Peter's Episcopal Church lambasted Gov. Ross Barnett as "a living symbol of lawlessness" and blamed the state's political leaders. The Rev. Murphey C. Wilds of

147

First Presbyterian focused on the rioters and "all who remained silent" when they should have spoken out against the violence. The Rev. Wayne Coleman of First Baptist called out his congregation "for not being the best of citizens," while the Rev. Roy A. Grisham at Oxford-University Methodist warned his congregants not to let "your conscience be your guide if it's too full of prejudice."[365]

A general assignment reporter, Gregory had a special connection with Ole Miss and Oxford. He grew up in Tupelo, just 30 minutes southeast of Oxford, and had earned bachelor's and master's degrees from Ole Miss. "I knew the area and it turned out to be a real plus during the week because I could very easily communicate with the university officials, the state officials. I was local. I wasn't one of these 'outside agitator' reporters,"[366] he recalled. Gregory identified with both sides of the conflict:

> There was sadness, amazement, feeling caught up in the moment. The student body enrollment wasn't much over 4,000 students, a very small campus. Everyone knew everybody. We had a championship football team and two Miss Americas there back to back. Here suddenly, the nation's press was descending on the campus along with 30,000 troops... The university was almost in, I don't want to say a lock-down, but just panic. There was this resentment that you could feel pervading everything with the administration, the townspeople, whatever. What the hell is going on—and this shouldn't be happening.[367]

Gregory was not in Oxford the night the riot broke out. Instead, he was sent to the Naval Air Station north of Memphis to verify rumors that troops were arriving while other *Commercial Appeal* reporters were sent to Oxford. At the Naval Air Station Gregory went to the Officers' Club:

> We had a great story, a scoop, really, about these troops mobilizing in Memphis for the incident that was maybe expected in Oxford. Of course, that story was completely forgotten four hours later and never made the press because events took over with the president on television and the movement of troops.[368]

Earlier *The Commercial Appeal* had assigned a Jackson-based reporter and other regional reporters to cover negotiations between Gov. Barnett and the Kennedys and subsequently to cover the riot. Gregory was dispatched to Mississippi Monday in the second wave of newsmen.

During the week Gregory interviewed faculty members and attended press briefings by Deputy Attorney General Nicholas Katzenbach and Assistant Attorney General John Doar. "The tear gas odor lingered. My eyes were burning even as I covered Katzenbach's press conference. He talked about what could happen and what the future would be. No one was happy about it."[369]

Returning to normal, Gregory wrote, included attending an upcoming football game between Ole Miss and the University of Houston. At first there was some confusion as to where the game would be played. It was announced that the game would be held on campus. Then, because Army troops were bivouacked on the playing field, the game was moved to Jackson. A special train was scheduled to take students to Jackson. Gregory wrote, "Gov. Barnett said he and private benefactors would pick up the tab for the trip." The headline read, "1200 Students Swapping Crisis for Grid Junket."[370] Students were mostly quite on the train, with little cheering and few festivities, except in one car dominated by a fraternity.

Gregory also visited an encampment in Lafayette County where units of the 108th Armored National Guard regiment were allowed to entertain their families. Family members spread picnic blankets and shared a meal with husbands and sweethearts. Soldiers were photographed with children on their shoulders.

However, Gregory found the servicemen had been ordered not to talk about their experiences. Speaking off the record, one guardsman observed, "I don't go much for that shooting and brickbat throwing." The Mississippi National Guard drew praise from regular army commanders for defending the federal marshals when the guardsmen were targets of the mob.

Gregory also reported on a group of Ole Miss professors who contradicted a university press statement blaming federal marshals for the riot. Gregory's headline read: "Professors Rally To Marshals' Side And Urge Inquiry." The professors stated that "it was unfair" and "almost completely false" to blame the riot on the marshals' presence. The University of Mississippi chapter of the American Association of University Professors drafted a resolution calling for an investigation by "the proper authorities."[371]

In part, the AAUP resolution stated that its members "believe in the use of courts and ballot boxes to state our convictions; we oppose and deplore the useless employment of clubs and missiles against fellow citizens in behalf of any convictions whatsoever. Riots, weapons and agitators have no place at a university . . .With the cooperation of the overwhelming majority of law-abiding Mississippi citizens, the University of Mississippi can return in the near future to the normal and peaceful conditions essential to education in Mississippi."[372]

The continuing saga of disgraced General Edwin Walker also ended in Oxford. Walker, who was arrested earlier in the week on federal charges of insurrection, conspiracy and seditious conspiracy, had been sent to a psychiatric hospital in Springfield, Missouri. The Federal Court in Oxford court ordered Walker released on a $50,000 bond and to seek psychiatric help. "Word had it," Gregory said, "that Walker's mother put up her silver and other valuables to raise her son's $50,000 bond."[373]

Walker's participation began even before Meredith's arrival in Oxford when he put out a call on the radio for a "volunteer army" of white supremacists to assemble at Ole Miss. The night of the riot, Walker stood on the base of the Confederate statue on the eastern edge of the Circle, seeking supporters. The statue, a duplicate of the one in front of the Lafayette County Courthouse, was dedicated in 1906 and bears the same inscription, honoring those who served.

According to the Rev. Duncan Gray, Walker encouraged the rioters in their assault of the Lyceum and told them that they had been "sold out" by Colonel T.B. Birdsong, the head of the Mississippi State Patrol. He was referring to Birdsong's troopers abandoning the campus earlier in the evening and then returning on orders of the governor.

Rev. Duncan Gray Jr., St. Peter's Episcopal Church

Pushing through Walker's supporters Gray struggled to the front and addressed the students, asking them to "behave like a human being, like the decent people that all of them were, and not like animals, and to get back to the dormitories."[374] He was pulled down from the monument, "shoved and hauled out to the sides of the crowd" where he was rescued.[375] English professor Evans Harrington, one of a small group of liberal faculty members at Ole Miss, was among those who came to his aid.[376]

Walker meanwhile, treated Gray's words with disdain, dismissing him: "And he is an Episcopal minister! It makes me ashamed to be an Episcopalian."[377]

As Gregory would learn, Gray, director of religious life at Ole Miss as well as rector of St. Peter's Episcopal Church, was not one to stand by passively. Gray made multiple forays to campus on the evening of September 30. His office was on the eastern edge of the Circle in the YMCA building, a campus recreation center and gathering place for religious groups.

The night of the riot the rectangular brick building also served as an infirmary. Social activities coordinator Louise Meadow, William Faulkner's sister-in-law, was pressed into service tending to bloodied rioters and injured newsmen. Rioters seeking bottles for Molotov cocktails had cleaned out the soda machine and there were no medical supplies in the facility. Meadow used paper towels as bandages and a pencil holder to hold water.

Earlier, after listening to President Kennedy's speech, Gray went to search for a faculty member he'd heard was injured. The man turned out to be fine, and assisted by the Rev. Wofford Smith, the campus chaplain, Gray asked students to give up their weapons. "We received considerable cooperation in this. Many of the students gave us their weapons and we took them back and threw them up against the Y wall as best we could... Only two or three resisted and refused at this point."[378]

Throughout the rest of the night, Gray tried to talk with students regarding their actions, collected more bricks and weapons, and finally went home around 11 p.m., weary and frustrated.

Gray had prepared his congregants for Meredith's arrival, delivering sermons as far back as February 1962.

St. Peter's Episcopal Church

A common theme ran through his sermons—preventing violence, upholding the law and treating Meredith as a person worthy of respect. He also organized an inter-faith committee that agreed on a common message: to "act in a manner consistent with the Christian teaching concerning the value and dignity of man" while "exerting whatever leadership and influence possible to maintain peace and order."[379]

In the weeks before the riot, Gray also served as a source for newsmen looking for knowledgeable, candid residents. Having the morning of September 30 preached a sermon instructing his congregation to accept the admission of Meredith "as the only practical and reasonable solution," Gray was high on the reporters' list of sources.

Two reporters who attended St. Peter's asked to interview Gray that afternoon, agreeing to meet at 2 p.m. The two reporters didn't show up, but a dozen others did. Gray asked them to wait for the men to arrive. The reporters grew restless. They knew something was going on but not where and what. The latest word was that Meredith would be registered at 10 a.m. the next morning. Where were the rival reporters? They pressed Gray if he knew where they might

James Meredith attending first class.

Photo by Ed Meek

have gone. He casually suggested they might be at the Oxford Airport watching the U.S. Marshals roll in. The reporters rushed to the airport. "Seems that none of the reporters had even listened to the radio to know what was going on,"[380] he joked later.

Hearst Headline News Service reporter John D. Harris knew what was going on. He was one of the reporters at the airport that afternoon observing families lined up on the airstrip "silent and grim-faced, some hefting clubs." He wrote of "a freckle-faced kid" asking his father: "What are those little containers the marshals are carrying in their pockets?" and his father's quiet reply, "Tear gas shells, son." And he described the "incredulous disbelief" on the faces of people lining the blacktop road leading to campus as they speculated about what lay ahead.[381]

Gregory, however, was not the only reporter to look to religion to get the measure of the community. On September 30, Hoke Norris of the *Chicago Sun-Times*, visited First Baptist Church, where the Rev. E. Wayne Coleman preached about an epistle written by Paul and, without specifically mentioning James Meredith, referenced, almost in passing, the events swirling outside the church's doors: "Man's institutions will change. Times changes everything… Change is the law of life. We resist it. We don't like it. But it is part of life."[382]

Afterwards, Coleman declined an interview regarding integration at Ole Miss, saying his concern was for the spiritual welfare of his congregants. His wife Margaret, however, was blunt: "Don't always judge people by their officials," Norris quoted her as saying. "Sometimes, we feel that it's all been taken out of our hands."[383]

A week after the riot, no new incidents were reported on the Ole Miss campus. Meredith was attending class, and integration was the new norm. After two deaths and over 160 wounded, including marshals and FBI agents, Mississippi had entered the mainstream.

WITHERING FIRE FROM PULPITS RAKES MISSISSIPPI'S DEFIANCE

The Commercial Appeal, October 7, 1962

by Neal Gregory

Oxford, Miss., October 7. – Church members of this university town knelt Sunday in a "day of repentance" for the violence and rioting that rocked Oxford and the University of Mississippi last week.

In almost every church the theme was the same: "We all share the guilt – this is a time for repentance."

At St. Peter's Episcopal church, the Rev. Duncan Gray, Jr., described Gov. Ross Barnett as "a living symbol of lawlessness" and declared that Mississippians have been "deceived and misled by their political leaders" since the Supreme Court handed down its school desegregation decree in 1954.

"The people of Mississippi were told by their leaders over and over again that the federal courts could be defied forever; that they would never have to obey the law of the land.... Is it any wonder, then, that violence erupts when the issue becomes real, rather then academic, within the borders of our own state?

"Think of the freshman and upperclassman as well who were out there throwing bricks and bottles the other night. Who could really blame them when the governor of the state himself was in open rebellion against the law, a living symbol of lawlessness?"

At First Presbyterian church, the Rev. Murphey C. Wilds said townspeople should repent for all those persons who produced the strife and "for all who remained silent when we should have spoken."

"There should be no resentment or bitterness toward those troops of the National Guard, many of whom we know, and the other troops we do not know, who brought order out of chaos and are maintaining that order."

The Rev. Wayne Coleman delivered a similar message at First Baptist Church, where he urged his congregation to be "thinking, reasonable people."

"We have sinned in not being the best of citizens, and not assuming our responsibility as citizens," said the Rev. Mr. Coleman. "We have not loved as well or done what God wants us to do."

"Laws we don't like are better than anarchy – insurrection and bloodshed – better than insecurity and fear."

At Oxford-University Methodist church, the Rev. Roy A. Grisham said the next generation of Mississippians would pay for the rioting and death which accompanied desegregation at Ole Miss.

"Every Mississippian is guilty for the situation we are in. Think about this. Pray about it. Take it seriously. Don't let your conscience be your guide if it's too full of prejudice.

"In my 30 years in the ministry, I have never faced a Sunday like today," the Rev. Mr. Grisham said. "We are in an ugly situation. We are not over it by any means. Do we have the calmness and boys to see it through?"

Military forces which arrived in Oxford last Monday to quell rioting caused by the enrollment of Negro James Meredith at the University of Mississippi continue to patrol the town and to check cars entering the nearby campus.

A few soldiers attended worship services in Oxford churches. Others participated in services conducted by Army chaplains at bivouac areas around the town.

Paul Guihard memorial bench installed by the campus chapter of the Society of Professional Journalists.

Photo by Larry Wells.

CONCLUSION

As faculty adviser to the University of Mississippi student chapter of the Society of Professional Journalists, I applied in 2009 for an SPJ grant to install a memorial bench in Paul Guihard's memory. Prominently situated at the Meek School of Journalism & New Media, the Guihard bench faces Sorority Row, the same street where the Army arrived in the early hours of October 1, 1962. Had he lived, Guihard most likely would have been near this street covering the story.

A year later, the Society of Professional Journalists named the Ole Miss campus a national historic site in journalism in honor of Paul Guihard and the 300-plus reporters who covered what is frequently called the last battle of the Civil War. It was the 100th historical designation made by SPJ.

Plaque designating the Ole Miss campus as a National Historic site in Journalism.
Photo by Larry Wells.

At the ceremonies marking the memorial, Hank Klibanoff, co-author of *The Race Beat*, called on "the killer of Paul Guihard, or anyone who knows the story of how Paul Guihard came to die on this campus, to come forward and tell the truth. Tell us what happened... Tell us your story... There are many people such as yourself carrying huge burdens, the burden of the long-lived lie that will be lifted when you tell the truth." Klibanoff also pleaded with family members who "may have heard stories about a relative being involved in the Guihard killing" to come forward if, for no other reason, to bring peace to Paul's family.[384] No one has come forward.

The FBI is still interested in the Guihard case, but, after 55 years, resolution may be difficult, if not impossible.

"It is never too late to do the right thing," said *Clarion-Ledger* reporter Jerry Mitchell at the dedication of the historic plaque. Mitchell, whose work has put four Klansmen behind bars, observed:

Freedom of the press is far from a privilege granted to a fortunate few. It is a sacred right given to all Americans. Throughout the centuries, freedom of the press has helped safeguard this nation from tyranny, from repression, and from those in government who scheme to keep us in the dark. We must not let this moment pass without noting that those involved in killing Paul Guihard walked free that day. They executed this international journalist within half a mile of hundreds of lawmen, scores of other reporters, and more than 2,000 students and civilians.[385]

CBS reporter Dan Rather, who also spoke at the plaque dedication, noted that the job of the reporter is to bear witness and "be an honest broker of information. To take the viewers to the scene . . .to get as close to the truth as you possibly can, recognizing that most of the time you can't get the truth, the whole truth, and nothing but the truth."[386]

Why do reporters do what they do? The easy answer is "it was my job," but that doesn't explain why a man or woman, not satisfied with reporting from a distance, decides to head toward danger. Psychiatric researcher Anthony Feinstein's 2004 study of journalists showed that both men and woman "eschew the nine-to-five routine and comfort of a predictable office job for the drama and excitement of the battlefield."[387] And what was the Ole Miss riot if not armed combat?

What Paul Guihard shared with the 300-plus reporters who covered the 1962 riot was the sense of mission described by Rather. Men and women are called to journalism, and, yes, it is a calling. Journalists speak for their communities and create public conversations. They don't set the agenda but give the public something to think about. In the process, they inspire communities to recognize their moral obligations. Community, in this context, extends beyond municipal boundaries just as Guihard's sacrifice, for example, forever links France and Mississippi. Journalists are reformers emboldened by the belief that stories, which shed light on public affairs and private discourse, can change the world.

Eventually, the reporters left Oxford and moved on to cover other stories. The Cuban Missile crisis occurred in late October 1962, turning the nation's attention away from the South and eastward toward the Soviet Union. Integration issues surfaced again when the University of Alabama was integrated in 1963 and when public school systems across the South began to move with "all deliberate speed" to obey the Supreme Court's orders to integrate. What until then had been solo events became a movement. The push for civil rights shifted from equal education toward voting rights, employment and housing issues.

Yet, though the newsmen and women who covered the Meredith crisis changed news organizations and/or moved up the professional ladder, none forgot the time they spent in Mississippi. Many, in fact, look back on Ole Miss as the highlight of their careers, a time when the press had a profound impact on a dramatic period of revolution in the 20th century. Their reporting helped galvanize public opinion and prod the government to enact, and enforce, laws to protect the rights of minorities and to dismantle segregation. Karl Fleming of *Newsweek* summed up the importance of reporting the Ole Miss crisis:

> I think we felt as much a commitment to what we were doing as to the movement itself, which is to say that despite the feelings, we managed to transmit just the facts. There was no need for any kind of flowery language. There was no need for excess. The facts were so horrific that they spoke for themselves... I remember a colleague of mine from *Newsweek*, Frank Trippet, who came from Mississippi. An aunt of his said, "Frank, you ain't going to start telling a lot of lies on us down there, are you?" And Frank said. "Well. I'm going to do worse than that; I'm going to tell the truth."[388]

When pushed, journalists will admit they entered the profession because of a desire to write for a living, the adrenalin rush of getting the story, the exhilaration of making deadline, of being in the front seat of events and informing their readers about events that impact their lives. But, at Ole Miss, there was something more. For most of the reporters, it was the first time they faced tear gas and flying bullets. It wasn't an assignment. It was a personal challenge.

Karl Fleming and Flip Schulke both survived brutal childhoods that made them pull for the underdog. Claude Sitton grew up with black playmates and believed African Americans were entitled to civil rights and equal opportunity. Fred Powledge headed south because the developing story was about his roots. Moses Newson, writing for the black press, approached stories as an activist who wanted to bring Meredith's quest to the attention of his readers. Dorothy Gilliam's goal was similar, but her goal was to educate the white readers of *The Washington Post* who had little idea of what life was like for African-Americans in the South. Gordon Yoder came to Oxford to document the news, but after the mob attacked him and his wife, they ended up being part of the story. Michael Dorman sought to define the mood of the South through the literary works of Faulkner. Neal Gregory went to Oxford's ministers for insights into the human condition. Richard Valeriani and Dan Rather experienced the raw power of broadcasting as a news medium. Sidna Brower, the petite editor of *The Mississippian*, stood up to the bullies on her campus and admonished them not to bring shame on the university.

Paul Guihard was part of that brotherhood.

At the cemetery in St. Malo, France, where Paul Guihard is buried, his brother Alain summed up how he wanted Paul to be remembered—as a newspaperman doing the job that he loved: "We have not forgotten and we will not forget you."[389]

The author and Alain Guihard walking in the cemetery at St. Malo where Paul Guihard is buried. Photo by Larry Wells.

AFTERWORD

Of the 18 daily newspapers in Mississippi, a slew of weeklies and a couple of competing broadcast outlets, few demonstrated objective views on segregation, or published stories rooted in journalism's ethical values when it came to desegregation. It took honest, and therefore jarring, reporting of northern media to awaken Mississippi to the reality within its own borders.

The state's newspapers and broadcast outlets, for the most part, were notorious for their insular attitudes and critical of anyone who dared to question the Southern views on race relations. Research by Susan Weill and Robert Hooker detailed the extent in which the state's news outlets failed to meet even the minimum effort to objectively report on civil rights issues. It is for that reason no Mississippi journalists are featured in the previous chapters.[390]

There were some notable exceptions and it is for that reason they are profiled in this chapter. Most are well known, a few are not. Three won Pulitzer Prizes. One left the state, no longer able to handle the threats to his person and business. Two were women, one of whom still practices aggressive journalism. These reporters, editors and publishers who dared to challenge the status quo faced cross burnings, economic boycotts and social ostracism.

For their fearless reporting and commitment to provide the public with the news in the face of personal and professional danger five are featured here. Included are: the Carter family, owners of *The Delta Democrat-Times* in Greenville; Hazel Brannon-Smith, editor and publisher of the *Lexington Advertiser;* Ira Harkey, editor and publisher of the *Pascagoula Chronicle*; Lucy Komisar, managing editor of the *Mississippi Free Press*, owned by the NAACP, and Bill Minor, who reported from Jackson for the *New Orleans Times-Picayune.*

Their work ran up against publishers and editors across the state who maintained a "vigilant guard over the racial, economic, political, and religious orthodoxy, of the closed society."[391] These editors belonged to the White Citizens Council, were members of the leading social and economic classes, and believed that God had ordained segregation for both white and black citizens. The newspapers listed the names of black citizens who tried to register to vote. Coverage of the black communities did not occur unless a crime was committed against a white person. Publishers used their influence to control state government. And so it went.

Objectivity was unknown in news columns and on the air even as the Hutchins Report called on newspapers to report the day's events in context, and with completeness.[392] Broadcast outlets censored newscasts that carried opposing views. Stories were framed in such a way as to blame outsiders. Mississippi newspapers, if they did cover civil rights events, tended to use wire service copy to distance themselves from the stories and to bury them. Locally written articles were heavily loaded with code words, emotional phrasing and semantic twists that cast a negative glow on the facts.[393]

The Mississippi press linked demands by the state's minority citizens to communism. Miscegenation was feared. And reports of violence against blacks were cast as public relations stunts designed to make whites look bad.

And as Dorothy Gilliam and Moses Newson have noted, white-owned newspapers in Mississippi during 1962 gave scant attention to news about black communities or citizens, and used news columns and editorials to campaign against desegregation, and especially Meredith's enrollment at Ole Miss.

It was, as Hooker concluded, easy to claim that the state press "slough(ed) its reporting and editorial responsibilities."[394]

Taking the lead were the newspapers with the largest circulation and political influence, *The Clarion-Ledger* and *Jackson Daily News*, whose reach extended from the newsroom to the statehouse and to Jackson's largest Baptist church. Their connections to Gov. Barnett also landed family members on state boards and commissions, extending their political and personal influence.[395]

Bill Minor, who started covering the state in 1947 for the *New Orleans Times-Picayune*, described the owners as "Bible-quotin', Bible-totin' racists."[396] Various researchers including Michael Patronik,

Gene Roberts and Hank Klibanoff support his view. The *Columbia Journalism Review*, in a 1967 article, called the newspapers "quite possibly the worst metropolitan newspapers in the United States."[397] Gene Roberts and Hank Klibanoff in *The Race Beat* said the Hedermans' biased coverage set a low standard that "editors at smaller papers found all too easy to meet."[398] Patronik, in his thesis *Newspaper Coverage of the Desegregation of Southern Universities*, found that *The Clarion-Ledger* "acted as a mouthpiece of the government, with the local papers falling into line."[399]

The *Clarion-Ledger*'s owners closely aligned themselves with Gov. Ross Barnett. The Jackson paper was unyielding in its opposition to desegregation on all fronts. It was negligent in its coverage of such an important in-state event. Reporting was left to wire services such as AP and UPI. The editors in Jackson often matched neutral wire stories with inflammatory headlines. On the occasions when the *Clarion-Ledger* devoted resources to in-house reporting, the results were very often unbalanced. They extensively quoted anti-integrationist government sources without counterbalancing views from parties in favor of desegregation. The editorial pages of the *Clarion-Ledger* acted as little more than sounding boards for readers and staff alike to express white supremacist, anti-government views... A full 95 percent of the editorial content was anti-desegregationist. It is not a stretch to imagine how the constant barrage of anti-segregationist sentiment spouting forth from the most influential newspaper in the Mississippi owned by one of the state's most influential families might set an agenda for resistance. Whatever the effect, it set a low bar for the rest of the newspapers in the state to aspire to. All but a few did.[400]

The Hederman family also controlled the state's largest television station, WLBT-TV. NBC producer Shad Northshield recalled that WLBT, the only network-affiliated station in Jackson, was called a tri-affiliate because it had arrangements with all three national networks—ABC, CBS and NBC—to air programming based on local preferences. WLBT was required by contract to open its newsroom to visiting network journalists seeking space to write and transmit stories. Northshield recalled one such visit:

> I remember in Jackson, I went there, and there were three tables against the wall in the newsroom. And this is the station, by the way, that lost its license— yeah, the worst—the worst case ever in the history of the FCC, but they had ABC, CBS, NBC, and it was so you each had a desk and it was "African Broadcasting Company, Colored Broadcasting System, Nigger Broadcasting Company" and they made the initial letters big but then hand written. And it wasn't some graffiti jerk. I mean this was the news director who as I remember was ... a member of the Citizens Council.
>
> Now, they also would say, "now that's the local news" at the end of their broadcasting. That's the local news produced by Mississippians in Mississippi and what you've heard is the truth. Now for the Yankee version, and now for another version, here is Huntley and Brinkley from New York City. And they cut their show a few seconds just to be sure to make it clear that this is those commie-carpetbaggers who are now going to present this.[401]

Hodding Carter III, whose family-owned *Delta Democrat-Times* in Greenville was known for its reporting on civil rights stories, said the Hedermans "were to segregation what Joseph Goebbels was to Hitler. They were cheerleaders and chief propagandists, dishonest and racist. They helped shape as well as reflect a philosophy which was, at its core, as undemocratic and immoral as any extant."[402]

The newspapers remained that way until leadership was passed to the next generation. Rea Hederman took over in the early 1970s and was working on a Pulitzer Prize-winning education series when the paper was sold to the Gannett Co. in 1982 for $110 million.[404]

Hodding Carter Jr.

Hodding Carter III, the second-generation Mississippi owner of *The Delta Democrat-Times*, inherited his progressive views from his father, "Big" Hodding Carter Jr. "Little Hodding" recalled that his strongest memory growing up was his father's admonition that "we had to be as directly involved in (the social changes) as we could possibly be, that this was a critical moment in our history."[405]

There was a general assumption at the beginning (in the 1950s) by a good part of the white leadership that in fact black Mississippians; black Southerners didn't really want the changes. That these were things that were being engineered and forced on the south by left wing agitators, outside forces; communist, Jewish intellectuals, whatever. There was a great sense of shock and some dismay in certain of those quarters when it turned out that blacks in fact thought that the 1954 decision ought to be implemented, that there ought to be changes, that the system didn't work. That it stunk.... What blacks thought however in Mississippi, in the 1950s was almost totally irrelevant, because there was no outside power to which they could sort of turn for assistance and there had not yet boiled up that absolute determination to seize the moment for themselves that you suddenly saw coming out of the kids starting in the early 1960s.[406]

Big Hodding acquired his liberal bent while a student at Bowdoin College in Maine, where he shared classrooms with blacks.[407] During his tenure at the paper, beginning in 1939, Carter used courtesy titles for African Americans, wrote editorials critical of the state's racist policies and actively supported Democratic politicians. He was hard-headed and labeled a firebrand, and was called other names, as he fought the state's racist policies. He won a Pulitzer Prize in 1946 for editorials critical of the treatment of Japanese-American soldiers received returning from World War II. On civil rights issues he began as a segregationist but over time his views evolved to a more moderate stance. He was an early critic of the White Citizens Councils but supported gradual integration of socity.

Hodding Carter III

Hodding III never planned on returning to Greenville from Princeton to work on the family paper. "I thought that being 'Little Hodding' was a terrible idea," he said. "But I did like seeing my name on a byline." [408] His goal was a job in the Foreign Service. After spending two summers on the *New Orleans Item* he was committed to journalism.

Taking control of *The Delta Democrat-Times* in 1959 while Big Hodding was in South Africa, Hodding III continued to uphold the liberal principles his father had established: "My position on racist demagoguery was clear, but no more clear than dad's position. Invoking racism was an evasion of dealing with the state's real problems. It (racism) was un-American and un-Christian, and had held the South down for decades."[409] Looking back much later, he explained:

> My life was a lot easier than most southern whites who consider themselves people of good will and trying to find a way out, because I had my father who had already established a position, which, while by Northern standards may have seemed conservative, by Mississippi standards seemed radical. So that when I came along, I already had that platform from which to change

and so I changed from 1959 when I came back to the paper as an editorial writer in what I was saying publicly, while I had already changed radically in what I felt privately. What I wrote increasingly came into correspondence with what I felt.[410]

The Society of Professional Journalism gave Hodding Carter III a national award in 1961 for editorials criticizing the Mississippi Legislature's eager endorsement of racist policies. As Mississippi conservatives erupted over the admission of James Meredith, Hodding III ramped up coverage and used editorials to educate and inform his readers.

On September 30, he dispatched a reporter to Oxford to cover unfolding events while *The Clarion-Ledger* and other newspapers relied on wire service reports. Hodding's September 30 editorial argued that Gov. Barnett had committed sedition for his role in the Meredith crisis, a position that inflamed many subscribers.

The reaction from the community was immediate and vicious, including death threats by phone and mail. Carter stashed guns in every room in his house, and family members stayed awake most of the night of September 30 alert for potential danger. "Crosses tended to be planted fast because it was known that there were guns at our place," Carter recalled.[411]

The following day the newspaper experienced a fifteen percent cancellation rate.[412] On the second night, while the Carters slept, a three-foot tall cross was burned on their property. "It turned out to be kids; and we would have killed them if they had come the night before, because we were just that primed up," he recalled.[413] Carter said he learned as a youth what it meant to have courage.

I have had the great fortune, not always fortune, sometimes something more painful than that, of growing up in my father's house. I had seen a man who I knew to be frightened, I knew hated the pressures, I knew felt besieged, nonetheless, tighten up his belt, and go out, and do what he thought was necessary. And I learned what courage was. It wasn't being a guy who's never afraid. Courage was being afraid and just saying, "Okay, you've got to go do it." I didn't always go do it. But it was also knowing that if you missed it one day or it missed it one week, then you had to get back up and go try it again. You know, I didn't spend my life coming along thinking that I was going to be out there fighting all the time, even though I was living in my father's house. But because I lived in my father's house, and because I followed in his footsteps, I knew that you could, that you could overcome it.[414]

Young Hodding served as assistant secretary of state for public affairs in President Jimmy Carter's administration and was the White House press secretary during the Iran hostage crisis. Subsequently he was a columnist with the *Wall Street Journal* and served as chief correspondent for "Frontline" on PBS. After heading the Knight Foundation, which raises money for journalism projects, Carter taught at The University of Maryland and the University of North Carolina.

Ira Harkey

Photo courtesy of the Harkey family

During World War II a bomb explosion that killed black and white sailors opened Ira Harkey's eyes to the senselessness of segregation, but it was not until his 1949 purchase of *The Chronicle* in Pascagoula that he became an advocate for integration in Mississippi. He began by using courtesy titles for African Americans, an act unheard of in Southern journalism.

Covering City Hall, Harkey also realized that blacks had little or no legal protection and newspapers contributed to their anonymity by not printing birth or death notices, or writing stories about social events and community concerns. He set out to change the newspaper and the community. Harkey banned the use of racial designations in news stories unless required for identification.

In print he is never a man. He is a Negro, negro or colored. His wife is not a woman. She is colored, Negro, negro or negress.

Indeed, she is not even allowed to be his wife in most Southern newspapers, being denied the title of Mrs. no matter how legally married she may be, and is referred to on the streets, in the courts and in the newspaper as Bessie Lou or Willie Mae or Mandy."[415]

Harkey was the first newspaper editor in Mississippi to support Meredith's enrollment application.[416] His editorials chided Gov. Ross Barnett's threats to close the university and the governor's opposition to federal intervention. Questioning the validity of the governor's positions, Harkey wrote in his September 18 editorial: "Governor Barnett knows full well how laws are enforced when the lawless are defiant. He himself has sent troops into counties to search out a bottle of whiskey here, to shatter a crap table there."[417]

His advocacy came with a price. The local sheriff organized a posse of men who traveled to Oxford and took part in the riot. Back home they continued to threaten and harass supporters of integration including Harkey. Meeting with impunity in the county courthouse the chartered organization numbered about 600 members. For four months *The Chronicle* was targeted. Death threats came by telephone. Hate mail arrived at the office. A cross was burned on Harkey's property. A rifle bullet penetrated the front doors. A shotgun blast tore through the office window. Advertisers faded away. Circulation dropped. Newspaper carriers were threatened.

The FBI launched an investigation after Claude Ramsay, president of the state AFL-CIO, reminded the union's members that racial unrest in Pascagoula could hurt employment at the nearby Ingalls shipbuilding plant. By August the membership of the Jackson County Citizens Emergency Unit had dwindled to about 22 members. But by then Harkey had sold the paper and enrolled in graduate school at The Ohio University. He explained:

> I could not remain in Pascagoula, could not bear to exist in the vacuum of ostracism that remained in force after victory, could not function in a silence of total isolation as if I were underwater or in galactic space. I had become an ambulatory and ubiquitous monument to the shame of my fellow townsmen, galling their late-blooming consciences.[418]

All told, Harkey endured 14 years of threats, criticisms, economic boycotts and social isolation for his progressive views and editorial policies that regarded the area's black citizens as equal to whites. Before he left, Harkey won a Pulitzer Prize for his editorials calling for the peaceful integration of the university. William Faulkner won his second Pulitzer for fiction the same year, giving Mississippi a significant boost in the literary world. "I wasn't surprised that the community or Mississippi newspapers didn't rejoice with me when I won the Pulitzer," he said. "I think they hated me even more for being recognized by the Yankees at Columbia University, whom they also called Communists."[419]

Tom Waring of the *Charlestown News and Courier* spoke for his peers in criticizing the award, noting that "A Mississippi editor who is out of step with Mississippi hardly could escape an award."[420] The *Columbia Journalism Review*, however, praised Harkey for his positions and courage.[421]

Harkey started his newspaper career at the *New Orleans Times-Picayune* after graduating from Tulane University. With the help of his father, a wealthy New Orleans businessman, he bought the small weekly on the Gulf Coast. "I had the dream that almost every city newspaperman had. He wanted to have a little weekly newspaper. He wanted to be the local oracle and run his own newspaper," Harkey recalled. "I had the feeling, and I hate to say this because I sound like a jerk, I had the feeling I could make a difference. That I could really teach these people that the black man was a human being and not an animal. That he deserved the same rights as everyone else."[422]

Equality was important to Harkey. It was a lesson he absorbed in Sunday School and at home where black employees were treated with dignity and respect. No negative words were allowed or tolerated. The lessons coalesced during his Navy service on the aircraft carrier USS Hancock during World War II when a 50-pound bomb exploded on deck, killing 52 sailors.

> As I watched the blur of canvas sacks slip over the side the conviction came to me that the Negro, who is good enough to be gutted by an unsegregated explosion, to be trussed in an

unsegregated sack, to be dumped into an unsegregated ocean and dispatched to an unsegregated heaven or hell, is just exactly good enough to live an unsegregated life in the nation of his birth.[423]

Hazel Brannon Smith

In 1964, *The Lexington Advertiser's* Hazel Brannon Smith became the first woman to win a Pulitzer for editorial writing for her editorials calling on fairness in civic affairs. The publisher of several weekly newspapers, Smith did not start out to challenge Jim Crow. She was a segregationist who believed in legal justice for all people, and this belief alone was enough to put her at odds with Mississippi leaders.

Aside from her position on integration issues, Smith's choice of a newspaper career, given her time and place, was remarkable. A working-class Alabama girl, Smith was born in 1914, a time of rigid social mores and strict segregation. But over 40 years, Smith moved from supportive of the separate-but-equal view decided by the U.S. Supreme Court in *Plessy vs Ferguson*, to one that advocated, not integration perhaps, but fairness to all citizens.[424]

Her advocacy and vision earned her the Pulitzer Prize while drawing the ire of the White Citizens Council and leading to a more than decade-long advertising boycott against the *Advertiser* beginning in 1960.[425] To Smith, the fear of change permeated the state's life:

Fear... hangs like a dark cloud over us, dominating every facet of public and private life. No one speaks freely anymore for fear of being misunderstood—editors, preachers, teachers and other professional people are affected by it as well as business and industry. Almost every man and woman is afraid to try to do

173

anything to promote goodwill and harmony between the races, afraid he or she will be taken as a mixer or worse.[426]

Smith began her career as a teen at the *Etowah Observer* in Gadsden, Alabama. She sold advertising and wrote some stories. After graduating in 1935 from the University of Alabama, where she served as managing editor of the university newspaper, she decided to start at the top, as a publisher, and bought the weekly *Durant News* (circ. 1,475) with a $3,000 loan. She later purchased two other newspapers, *The Northside Reporter* in Jackson and the *Banner County Outlook* in Flora, as well as *The Advertiser* in Lexington (circ. 2,800).[427]

Smith was outspoken and flamboyant in dress and style. She wore large hats, drove a convertible, built a mansion that resembled Tara in *Gone with the Wind*, and entertained lavishly.[428] She used her newspapers' stories, editorial pages and her column to call local officials to task. Initially, her focus was local corruption beginning with a campaign in 1946 against slot-machine operators and bootleggers.[429] She later shifted to civil rights. Her editorial philosophy rested on her belief in Christian fairness and the moral fundamentalism that characterizes American Progressivism.[430]

Even though her newspapers were small weeklies, her stories were noticed. A complaint made to the state Sovereignty Commission described her as "this female crusading scalawag domiciled in our midst."[431]

Her fiery columns and editorials during the Meredith crisis alienated her from her peers. She called for Gov. Ross Barnett's resignation, writing: "The course he seems determined to follow through to the bitter end is one of continued resistance, which means he will have placed our state in a lawless position of promoting anarchy. And we will be thus regarded throughout the world."[432] She followed it up with reprints of news dispatches critical of Mississippi from around the world.[433]

After Meredith was enrolled, she took to task parents, newspaper editors, religious institutions as well as the state's "lawyers, judges and respected men," who declined to speak up on behalf of law and order.[434] In its story on Smith's having won the Pulitzer Prize, *Time* magazine noted:

> Mrs. Smith couldn't be more unpopular in Mississippi if she were an integrationist, which she isn't. But she is the next best thing. Her papers and her editorials have fearlessly called for reason on the race issue, whether she is challenging the White Citizens Council ("If they have their way, the free press in Mississippi will be destroyed, and with it the liberty and freedom of all Mississippians"), or reporting a concert by Metropolitan Opera Star Leontyne Price in Laurel, where Miss Price was born ("Leontyne does not need Mississippi, but Mississippi needs Leontyne").[435]

Her positions wreaked havoc on her personal and professional life. Her husband lost his job as administrator at the county hospital in 1960. In 1961, within a year of the Citizens Council boycott, *The Advertiser* was $55,000 in debt.[436] The debts increased over the years, eventually leading to bankruptcy. The Sovereignty Commission also criticized her for publishing issues of the NAACP-owned *Mississippi Free Press*, which she printed to earn income.[437]

There were cross-burnings on her lawn and death threats. *The Jackson Reporter* office was bombed in 1964. Arsonists set fire to *The Advertiser's* printing press in 1967. Smith remained strong and committed, writing in her column: "When I am no longer free to print the truth unafraid, then you are no longer free to speak the truth without fear." [438]

Bill Minor

The same courage surfaced in Bill Minor's hardscrabble Depression childhood and military service as gunnery officer on a destroyer in the Pacific. World War II gave Minor a toughness that he used to confront politicians and civic leaders on both sides of the aisle.

Minor's deep knowledge of Mississippi politics made him a source for out-of-state reporters. Noted Minor, "My own situation in those civil rights decades was a unique one. I was something of a war correspondent behind enemy lines covering the battle of blacks to achieve first-class citizenship."[439] Joseph B. Cumming Jr., *Newsweek*'s Atlanta bureau chief during the period, observed, "Minor was the only good reporter in Mississippi during those crucial, historic years... (He was) in position to report consistently and aggressively and honestly in the local press what was going on in the controversial racial story of the 1960s."[440]

Minor's connections to the State House gave him access to transcripts of the secret negotiations between Gov. Barnett and Attorney General Robert F. Kennedy that preceded the 1962 riot. According to a subsequent *Newsweek* article, the tapes "gave a fascinating view of men in power trying to accommodate to political reality."[441]

On the tapes, Kennedy can be heard telling Barnett about the decision to mobilize the Mississippi National Guard, and President Kennedy's threat to reveal on national television their secret negotiations to resolve the crisis. The Kennedy White House used the tapes as a hammer over Barnett's head to accomplish Meredith's enrollment. Barnett feared having their conversations made public. His capitulation, however, opened the door to armed resistance.

In explaining the extent of Minor's abilities, Jack Nelson, Atlanta bureau chief for the *Los Angeles Times* in the 1960s, recalled:

No reporter covering the South in those days, including myself, would have thought of going to Mississippi to cover a major story, whether on politics, economics, or civil rights without checking with a man we all recognized as an expert, Bill Minor. He could tell you who was in the Klan or was sympathetic. He could tell you how much the Klan had infiltrated the state police or the governor's office. He knew who to talk to and who not to talk to.[442]

Minor's byline appeared in *Newsweek*, The Associated Press, *The New York Times*, *New Republic*, *The Herald Tribune*, among other national publications. Praise of Minor's unflinching view of the state came at a cost. No paper nominated him for a Pulitzer Prize, nor did he receive any other major journalism award in that period.

Mississippi journalism in the 1960s was often marked by personal relationships between reporters and politicians. It was an old boy's club where reporters rode with elected officials, shared meals and drinks, and practiced a form of journalism that separated the private lives of politicians from their public personas. Jerry Mitchell, civil rights reporter for *The Clarion-Ledger*, tells the little known story of one of Minor's early encounters with Barnett that says a great deal about life in rural Mississippi:

When Ross Barnett ran for governor for the first time, in 1951, Minor drove to cover his speech in Cleveland. Afterwards, Barnett, who was with his wife and three children, turned to Minor and asked, "Bill, you think I can find a place to stay?" Minor told Barnett he was welcome to stay with him if he couldn't find another place. He forgot about the offer and awoke at 1 a.m. to a knock on the door. Not only was Barnett standing there. So were his son and sound-truck driver. "We had to decide who would sleep with who, and I picked Ross," Minor said. "He never thanked me for taking him in."[443]

This may seem improbable until viewed in the context of the times. Few hotels dotted the rural Mississippi landscape and Mississippians were hospitable even to those they disliked, hence Minor's willingness to offer lodging to a political candidate.

Photo courtesy of Lucy Komisar.

Lucy Komisar

Lucy Komisar, a junior at Queens College, arrived in Jackson two weeks before James Meredith enrolled in The University of Mississippi. Her goal was to write for the *Mississippi Free Press*, a weekly newspaper financed by the Mississippi NAACP chapter and civil rights activists. Its mission was to inform the state's black citizens about voting rights issues. Traveling from New York to Mississippi on a Greyhound bus, Komisar soon noticed signs at bus terminals designating separate drinking fountains for whites and blacks. Her mission to report discrimination had begun.[444]

The only daughter of politically inactive New Yorkers, Bronx-born Komisar was on track to become a high school teacher of Spanish or French. She had graduated fourth in her high school class in Valley Stream, Long Island. For bright girls in 1959 the options were often limited to careers in education or nursing as there were few role models in other professional fields much less opportunities for employment. Her family-life was traditional—for the most part her mother stayed at home (Komisar also had two brothers) and her father worked as a salesman for a canning company. Her grandparents had emigrated from Russia but the family were non-practicing Jews and religion played little role, if any, in her commitment to social justice.

It was while a freshman at Queens College, part of the city's free college network, that Komisar's life opened up as she took advantage of the rich culture life and educational opportunities offered by the college. Attending a current events colloquium at Yale University in March 1960, Komisar heard a presentation by civil rights activist Allard Lowenstein, who spoke about the recent lunch counter sit-in at a Woolworth's lunch counter in Greensboro, N.C.[445] For Komisar this was a call to action: "The sit-ins had just started a month before.

It was a very dramatic occurrence and very moving. There were several hundred of us at the conference to talk about current events; it wasn't just about the sit-ins. But he was there, and got many of us involved. From then on, I was involved in the civil rights movement.[446]

Absorbing Lowenstein's passion, Komisar joined the Young People's Socialist League, the Queens College chapter of the NAACP and the National Student Association. She then began her career advocating for reform and attended the formative meeting of the Student Non-violent Coordinating Committee. SNCC became a major force in the Freedom Rides and early civil rights activities. A year later, as an YPSL volunteer staff member she participated in a sit-in in New York in support of movie theater desegregation efforts in Texas.

In early 1962 she was arrested in Elkton, Maryland, for entering a restaurant with a black friend seeking to be served. Her presence in Maryland stemmed from her participation in the U.S. 40 Freedom Rides, which sought to desegregate buses as well as restaurants, bowling alleys and drugstores.[447] "I thought then, I'm going to have to decide now for the rest of my life that I will do what I believe in and not be silenced by fear of not getting a job. I decided though it may well have had consequences."[448]

In the summer of 1962, Komisar said she yearned to do more than participate in sit-ins. A chance meeting with one of the founders of the *Free Press* at the annual Midwest meeting of the National Students Association led Komisar to head to Mississippi. William Higgs, the white Mississippi lawyer who helped found the *Free Press*, wanted to use the newspaper "to secure these (freedom of speech, worship, movement, and freedom from intimidation) freedoms for those Mississippians who have been denied them."[449] Komisar had little experience beyond working on her high school and college newspapers, and Brenda Starr on her mind.[450] "I decided to go to Mississippi. I took a leave of absence from school. That was in August, and a month later, I took a bus to Mississippi."[451]

Editor Charles Butts recalled that Komisar did not contact him before she arrived by bus: "she just got on the bus and came... (deciding) this is where she had to be." He said Komisar was "very-self assured" and a "strong woman when that was not as common." "You don't see that as often as you do today, particularly among women of that age. She was not even old enough to vote. You had to be 21."[452] Komisar said she "soon became editor in name as well as a fact as Charlie focused on raising money for the operation and writing the editorials."[453]

The job had its dangers: The two journalists made sure they were never alone in the office and lived in separate furnished apartments in the white part of Jackson because "we were putting out a newspaper that did not make us very popular with segregationist whites," Komisar recalled. "We would just do our jobs. Our paper would be published and we would go around town and talk to people who we had to talk to. We were not going to give them any reason to light a fire, in that respect we had to be very circumspect."[454] The pair received no salary, only food and rent money of about $20 a week.[455] Komisar added that she felt "welcome and safe in the black part of Jackson and somewhat alienated from the white part, and a bit nervous there."[456]

Although she never directly experienced danger or physical assault, Komisar was aware that her presence, and the newspaper, was not welcomed in the white community. "I would go to the people I needed to interview, and then would go home. I didn't go wandering around at night myself. I would just go home. What else would I do? I had to be in the black part of town to do the stories, and then I lived in the white part of town."[457]

When Meredith was admitted to the university Komisar was holed up in the *Mississippi Free Press* office." I was writing the whole paper and we didn't have the luxury to send reporters. I would have had to go by bus," she recalled. "It was a question of logistics."[458]

Instead, Komisar, whose official title was managing editor, relied on telephone interviews to write the story.[459] Yet despite her contention that no *Free Press* reporters were sent to Oxford, the October 6, 1962 issue included a first-person account of the riot and its aftermath.[460] The story carries no byline as was typical of stories published in the paper. Butts said because the staff consisted of only two people "we would incorporate conversations with people to get reports."[461]

Meanwhile, the forces behind the *Free Press* did not go unnoticed in Mississippi. The paper was the brainchild of Medgar Evers, the NAACP activist murdered in Jackson in 1963. Evers wanted a vehicle to communicate civil rights news to the state's black citizens.[462] Joining Higgs as founder on the HiCo (an acronym for Hinds County, the newspaper's home county) incorporation papers was the Rev. Robert L.T. Smith Jr., an African-American running for Congress, the future head of the Mississippi Democratic Freedom Party and the owner of Smith's Grocery. The newspaper's offices were in a back room at the grocery. All board members were African-American.[463]

Butts noted that Smith's candidacy gained legitimacy because it had the backing of a newspaper.[464] While the paper's circulation was small it attracted enough readers to be ranked third in the state in terms of circulation (with an estimated circulation of 40,000) behind *The Clarion-Ledger* and *Jackson Daily News*.[465] Butts noted: "that tells you how illiterate and unread they were" in Mississippi.[466] Subscribers hailed from the state's rural population and the newspaper was distributed through the mail. "Back then weekly newspapers could be circulated for a fraction of a cent, as long as you were a

James Meredith, right, and son John attend the Meredith statue
commemoration at the University of Mississippi.
Photo by Robert Jordan, University of Mississippi Communications Department.

newspaper, as long as a subscribed newspaper."[467] The paper cost one dollar for 52 issues.

Komisar spent a year in Mississippi, returning to New York in August 1963 after participating in the 1963 Freedom March in Washington, D.C. After graduation Komisar landed a job as a newsroom assistant at the *New York Post* and when she could not get promoted to a newspaper job launched her career as a feminist, serving one term as vice president of the National Organization of Women. She also went on to a successful career as a political organizer, investigative journalist, book author and freelance writer, focusing on social and political issues.

According to Butts, Komisar was "young enough not to know what the adults knew. The adults knew you could not persuade a giant and you couldn't do those kinds of things, and she went and did them."[468]

APPENDIX

WHL: CJS

1

LIST OF NEWS REPRESENTATIVVES AT OXFORD, MISSISSIPPI

On October 22, 1962, EDWIN GUTHMAN, Special Assistant for the Public Information, U.S. Department of Justice, Washington, D.C., furnished the Federal Bureau of Investigation with a partial list of news reporters who were at Oxford, Mississippi, some time during the crisis surrounding the efforts of JAMES H. MEREDITH to enroll in the University of Mississippi. It will be noted that 31 names appearing on the list furnished by Mr. GUTHMAN did not appear on one list of newsmen registered at the University of Mississippi during the period September 18, 1962, and October 1, 1962, as made available by GEORGE STREET, Assistant to the Director of Development, University of Mississippi, as set out elsewhere in this report.

This list furnished by Mr. GUTHMAN is as follows:

LIST OF NEWS REPRESENTATIVES AT OXFORD, MISSISSIPPI

On October 20, 1962, Mr. GEORGE STREET, Assistant to the Director of Development, University of Mississippi, Oxford, Mississippi, made available to SA ROBIN O. COTTEN a list of news representatives who registered at the University of Mississippi between September 18, 1962, and October 1, 1962, which list is as follows:

	DATE REGISTERED	NAME	NEWS MEDIA	HOME ADDRESS
(1)	9/20/62	ABERNATHY, HARRY B.	Press Register	Clarksdale, Mississippi
(2)	9/20/62	ALEXANDER, STEVEN	KTAL-TV	Shreveport, Louisiana
(3)	No date	ALLEN, CHUCK	WLBT-TV	Jackson, Mississippi
(4)	No date	ANDERSON, JOHN K.	KAAY	Little Rock, Arkansas
(5)	9/20/62	ANGELO, BONNIE	Newsday	Washington, D. C.
(6)	9/20/62	ATKINS, JIM	WBRC-TV	Birmingham, Alabama
(7)	9/20/62	AYCOCK, EARL	Radio WDAL	Meridian, Mississippi
(8)	9/28/62	BAKER, ROBERT E. L.	Washington Post	Washington, D. C.
(9)	9/28/62	BARTSCH, GEORGE F.	Associated Press	Little Rock, Arkansas
(10)	No date	BAXTER, GORDON F.	KTRM	Beaumont, Texas
(11)	9/27/62	BEATTY, BILL	Canadian Broadcasting Corp.	Toronto, Canada

183

(12)	No date	BELTZ, TOM	KYW-Cleveland, Ohio	Cleveland, Ohio
(13)	9/21/62	BENTON, NELSON	CBS News	New York City, New York
(14)	No date	BEST, CORT	Courier Journal	Louisville, Kentucky
(15)	9/20/62	BINGHAM, CLIFF	WLBT-TV	Jackson, Mississippi
(16)	9/18/62	BIRD, ROBERT S.	New York Herald Tribune	New Orleans, Louisiana
(17)	9/29/62	BISHOP, BOB	WRBC Jackson	Jackson, Mississippi
(18)	No date	BOGGS, NEIL	NBC News	Chicago, Illinois
(19)	9/25/62	BOHN, CHARLES A., JR.	KMOX-TV	St. Louis, Missouri
(20)	9/20/62	BONDS, R. J.	WBIP	Booneville, Mississippi
(21)	9/18/62	BOURDIER, JAMES A.	Associated Press	New Orleans, Louisiana
(22)	9/29/62	BOURQUIN, ELISABETH	France-Suir	New York City New York
(23)	9/26/62	BRANDON, HENRY	London Sun Times	Washington, D. C.
(24)	9/19/62	BREWER, NORMAN	WMCT	Memphis, Tennessee
(25)	9/19/62	BROWN, HARRY	CBS	Jackson, Mississippi
(26)	9/28/62	BRUBAKER, HERBERT M.	Radio Press International	Washington, D. C.
(27)	No date	BRYANT, W. W.	WGBA Radio	Columbus, Georgia
(28)	No date	BULBECK, JOHN	Reuters Ltd.	New York City New York
(29)	9/18/62	BURNS, BILLY	WSUH	Oxford, Mississippi
(30)	9/20/62	BUSH, KENNETH	Press Register	Clarksdale, Mississippi
(31)	9/19/62	CADWELL, CHARLIE	WMCT	Memphis, Tennessee
(32)	9/20/62	CALDWELL, H. M.	Daily Star	Grenada, Mississippi
(33)	9/18/62	CAMPBELL, LESLIE C.	Radio Station WSUH	Oxford, Mississippi
(34)	9/26/62	CAPART, BOB	Delta Democrat Times	Greenville, Mississippi
(35)	9/28/62	CHAMPION, RALPH	London Daily Mirror	New York City New York
(36)	9/29/62	CLABBY, BILL	Wall Street Journal	Dallas, Texas
(37)	9/19/62	CLARK, ROBERT E.	ABC	Washington, D. C.
(38)	9/19/62	CLAYTON, JAMES	Washington Post	Arlington, Virginia
(39)	9/28/62	COFFEY, RAY	Chicago Daily News	Chicago Illinois
(40)	9/20/62 9/25/62	COLEMAN, WAYNE	WTUP	Tupelo, Mississippi
(41)	No date	CONSIDINE, BOB	Hearst Papers	New York City New York
(42)	9/28/62	CRIDER, W. C.	Associated Press	Memphis, Tennessee
(43)	No date	CUMMINGS, JOE	Newsweek	Atlanta, Georgia

(44)	9/24/62	CUNNINGHAM, PAUL J.	NBC News	New York City New York
(45)	9/19/62	DABBS, WALLACE	Commercial Dispatch	Columbus, Mississippi
(46)	9/28/62	DANCY, BUD	Westinghouse Broadcasting Co.	Cleveland, Ohio
(47)	9/20/62	DANIEL, LEON	United Press International	Atlanta, Georgia
(48)	9/26/62	DAVIS, JAMES	CBS News	St. Petersburg, Florida
(49)	9/28/62	DEAN, NORMAN	Birmingham News	Birmingham, Alabama
(50)	9/27/62 9/28/62	DEARMAN, STANLEY (STAN)	Meridian Star	Meridian, Mississippi
(51)	9/28/62	DECKARD, JAMES F.	KTAL-TV	Shreveport, Louisiana
(52)	No date	DEVINE, FRANCIS	Australian newspaper	New York City, New York
(53)	9/25/62	DILTAND, LARRY N.	WNAU	New Albany, Mississippi
(54)	9/27/62	DIXON, KENNETH LEE	Meridian Star	Meridian, Mississippi
(55)	9/18/62	DONALDSON, GORDON	Toronto Telegram	Toronto, Ontario
(56)	9/28/62	DORMAN, MICHAEL	Newsday	Garden City, New York
(57)	9/28/62	DUKE, BILL	KRLD-TV	Dallas-Ft. Worth, Texas
(58)	No date	ECHEVERRIA, TED	Tribune	Covington, Louisiana
(59)	9/28/62	ELLIOTT, DON	WLBT-TV	Jackson, Mississippi
(60)	No date	ELLIS, CRAIG	Nashville Banner	Nashville, Tennessee
(61)	9/20/62	EVANS, G. V.	WBRC	Birmingham, Alabama
(62)	No date	FAURE, BRUCE	Tribune	Covington, Louisiana
(63)	9/18/62	FELLOWS, BOB	Life	Tampa, Florida
(64)	No date	FENDALL, YERXA	ABC	New York City New York
(65)	No date	FERGUSON, HARRY	United Press International	Washington, D. C.
(66)	9/19/62	FLEMING, KARL	Newsweek	Atlanta, Georgia
(67)	9/28/62	FOLSOM, BILL	WFAA-TV	Dallas, Texas
(68)	9/28/62	FORMAN, HY	KSLA-TV	Shreveport, Louisiana
(69)	9/28/62	FOSTER, W. R.	WDSU-TV	New Orleans, Louisiana
(70)	No date	FRERCK, WALT	United Press International	Little Rock, Arkansas
(71)	9/26/62	FRUZIER, WILSON	WHSX Radio	Hattiesburg, Mississippi
(72)	No date	GAST, JOE A.	KFDA-TV	Amarillo, Texas
(73)	No date	GLUCKS, JIM	Scripps Howard	Washington, D. C.
(74)	No date	GOLDMAN, PETER L.	Newsweek	New York City, New York
(75)	9/28/62	GORDON, WILLIAM M.	Newark News	Newark, New Jersey

(76)	9/20/62	GRAFFIA, JOE	WNOE	New Orleans, Louisiana
(77)	9/19/62	GREEN, JERRY	WMPS	Memphis, Tennessee
(78)	9/18/62	GREGORY, NEAL	Commercial Appeal	Memphis, Tennessee
(79)	9/28/62	GREGORY, TOM	Meridian Star	Meridian, Mississippi
(80)	No date	GREIDER, BILL	Louisville Times	Louisville, Kentucky
(81)	9/28/62	GRIFFETH, FRED J.	Commercial Appeal	Memphis, Tennessee
(82)	9/25/62	GROVE, GRAHAM	ABC	New York City, New York
(83)	9/24/62	GUENETTE, ROBERT	CBS News	New York City, New York
(84)	9/29/62	GWIN, JOHNNY	WDDT	Greenville, Mississippi
(85)	9/18/62	HALL, WEBBER	ABC News	Memphis, Tennessee
(86)	No date	HARGRODER, CHARLES	Times Picayune	Baton Rouge, Louisiana
(87)	No date	HARPER, J. E.	NBC	New York City, New York
(88)	9/29/62	HARRIGAN, ANTHONY	Charles S. C. News & Courier	Charleston, South Carolina
(89)	No date	HARRIS, JOHN	Hearst Papers	New York City, New York
(90)	No date	HATCH, RICHARD W.	United Press International	Nashville, Tennessee
(91)	9/26/62	HAYNES, GARY	United Press International Newspictures	Atlanta, Georgia
(92)	9/20/62	HEATON, KEITH	Movietonews	Miami, Florida
(93)	9/27/62	HERBERT, NICHOLAS	London Times	Washington, D. C.
(94)	9/19/62	HESTON, BEATRICE	Fairchild Publications	Palm Beach, Florida
(95)	9/26/62	HICKMAN, DON	WMCT News	Memphis, Tennessee
(96)	9/29/62	HICKS, JIMMY	Life	Houston, Texas
(97)	No date	HIRSCH, JACK	NBC	New Orleans, Louisiana
(98)	9/19/62	HODGKINS, HOWARD	United Press International	Washington, D. C.
(99)	9/28/62	HODGSON, GODFREY	London Observer	Washington, D. C.
(100)	9/19/62	HOFFMAN, WENDELL	CBS News	Manhattan, Kansas
(101)	9/27/62	HOLLADAY, ED	WOKK	Meridian, Mississippi
(102)	9/29/62	HOLLAND, CECIL	Washington Star	Washington, D. C.
(103)	9/19/62	HUFF, JERRY W.	United Press International	Nashville, Tennessee
(104)	9/28/62	JAMES, GEORGE	Time Magazine	Washington, D. C.
(105)	9/19/62	JAMES, WALTER, JR.	CBS News	Arabi, Louisiana
(106)	9/18/62	JOHNSON, J. W. (SKIP)	Associated Press	Mobile, Alabama

(107)	9/20/62	JONES, BOB	KNOG News	Monroe, Louisiana
(108)	9/29/62	JORDAN, FRANK	NBC News	Chicago, Illinois
(109)	9/29/62	JOYCE, THOMAS H.	Washington Bureau, Detroit News	Silver Spring, Maryland
(110)	9/26/62	JUMPER, DEXTER	WTUP Radio	Tupelo, Mississippi
(111)	9/20/62	KELLEY, ROGER	KNOG News	Monroe, Louisiana
(112)	9/28/62	KILPATRICK, JAMES J.	Richmond News Leader	Richmond, Virginia
(113)	9/18/62	KILPATRICK, LEROY	WSUH	Oxford, Mississippi
(114)	9/19/62	KINGSLEY, JAMES D.	Commercial Appeal	Memphis, Tennessee
(115)	No date	KIRKMAN, JAY	KFDA-TV	Amarillo, Texas
(116)	9/28/62	KLUEHE, HAL	NBC News	Chicago, Illinois
(117)	No date	KOENENN, JOSEPH C.	Commercial Appeal	Memphis, Tennessee
(118)	No date	KOKOJAN, HENRY A.	Sims Assoc.	Dallas, Texas
(119)	No date	KOLENOVSKY, ED F.	Associated Press	Houston, Texas
(120)	9/19/62 9/28/62	KUETTNER, AL	United Press International	Atlanta, Georgia
(121)	9/20/62	LALA, LARRY	WWL-TV	New Orleans Louisiana
(122)	9/20/62	LALA, MIKE	WDSU-TV	New Orleans Louisiana
(123)	9/26/62	LANGFORD, C. L.	Bolivar Commercial	Cleveland, Mississippi
(124)	9/28/62	LANKFORD, TOM	Birmingham News	Birmingham, Alabama
(125)	No date	LARN, HUBERT	?	Sweden
(126)	No date	LAUGHLIN, WILLIAM	NBC	New Orleans Louisiana
(127)	9/27/62	LAXSON, JIM	Associated Press	Atlanta, Georgia
(128)	9/20/62	LEAPTROTT, WILLIAM	Memphis Press Scimitar	Memphis, Tennessee
(129)	9/28/62	LE BRETON, EDMOND	Associated Press	Washington, D. C.
(130)	No date	LEVITON, JAY B.	Time Magazine	Atlanta, Georgia
(131)	9/28/62	LOVELL, JAN A.	KTBS-TV	Shreveport, Louisiana
(132)	9/19/62	LYON, FRED W., JR.	United Press International	Atlanta, Georgia
(133)	9/18/62	MC AFEE, BILL	CBS News	Memphis, Tennessee
(134)	9/20/62	MC BRIDE, MIKE	WTUP	Tupelo, Mississippi
(135)	9/21/62	MC CARLEY, HAL	WBLE	Batesville, Mississippi
(136)	9/29/62	MC COY, DAN	Black Star	Houston, Texas
(137)	9/28/62	MC GRATH, E. G.	Boston Globe	Boston, Massachusetts

(138)	9/29/62	MC GREGOR, BOB	WRBC Jackson	Jackson, Mississippi
(139)	9/19/62	MC INTOSH, ROBERT J.	WKDL	Clarksdale, Mississippi
(140)	No date	MC NEANS, ERNEST	Globe Photos	Huntsville, Alabama
(141)	9/29/62	MC NENLY, PAT	Toronto Star	Toronto, Canada
(142)	9/19/62	MARLIN, CAL A.	NBC News	Miami, Florida
(143)	9/29/62	MARTIN, RICHARD	WQIC	Meridian, Mississippi
(144)	No date	MASSIE, ROBERT K.	Saturday Evening Post	White Plains, New York
(145)	9/28/62	MATHEWS, BOB E.	KWTV Ch. 9	Oklahoma City, Okla.
(146)	No date	MATHIAS, PAUL	Paris ?	Paris, France
(147)	9/28/62	MAUGHAN, GENE	WRAG	Carrollton, Alabama
(148)	9/20/62	MEIGHAN, PAUL	KTAL-TV	Shreveport, Louisiana
(149)	9/18/62	METZ, GEORGE	Birmingham News	Meridian, Mississippi
(150)	No date	MICHEL, LYNN	NBC	New Orleans, Louisiana
(151)	9/20/62	MILES, BILL	Daily Journal	Tupelo, Mississippi
(152)	No date	MILLER, FRANCIS	Life	Chicago, Illinois
(153)	9/18/62	MILLINER, LOUIS	Associated Press	New Orleans, Louisiana
(154)	9/19/62	MOFFITT, DONALD A.	Wall Street Journal	Dallas, Texas
(155)	9/18/62	MOORE, CHARLES	Black Star Photo Agy.	Montgomery, Alabama
(156)	9/18/62	MOORE, E. P., JR.	Commercial Appeal	Greenville, Mississippi
(157)	9/19/62	MOORE, JOE	Clarion Ledger	Jackson, Mississippi
(158)	No date	MORELOCK, M. J.	WAAX	Gadsden, Alabama
(159)	No date	MORIN, R. G.	Associated Press	New York City New York
(160)	9/28/62	MOSELEY, JOHN T.	Shreveport Times	Shreveport, Louisiana
(161)	9/28/62	NEAL, BRUCE	The Mayes Stations	Ft. Worth, Texas
(162)	9/26/62	NELSON, ROBERT	Christian Science Monitor	Chicago, Illinois
(163)	9/20/62	NICHOLAS, WILLIAM	Jackson Daily News	Jackson, Mississippi
(164)	9/19/62	NOEL, EDMUND	Clarion Ledger	Jackson, Mississippi
(165)	9/19/62	NORRIS, DUDLEY E.	Time	Atlanta, Georgia
(166)	9/28/62	OPOTOWSKY, STAN	New York Post	New York City New York
(167)	No date	OTTO, LOWELL	NBC	New Orleans, Louisiana
(168)	9/19/62	OWENS, (?) M.	NBC News	Miami, Florida
(169)	No date	PAPPAS, I. W.	WNEW	New York City, New York

(170)	9/27/62	PENDERGAST, TOM	Associated Press	New York New Orleans, Louisiana
(171)	No date	PENOT, THEODORE	NBC	New Orleans, Louisiana
(172)	No date	PEQUEGNAT, PAUL	Canadian Broadcasting Corp.	Ottawa, Canada
(173)	9/29/62	PHILLIPS, JOHN M.	New York Times	New York City, New York
(174)	9/26/62	PIERCE, LAURENS	CBS News	Montgomery, Alabama
(175)	No date	PIPES, RICHARD	Amarillo Globe News	Amarillo, Texas
(176)	9/28/62	PLANER, ED	WDSU-TV	New Orleans, Louisiana
(177)	9/18/62	PORTEOUS, CLARK	Press Scimitar	Memphis, Tennessee
(178)	9/27/62	POWELL, BRUCE	NBC-TV	Chicago, Illinois
(179)	No date	POWELL, CLAUDE	Associated Press	Jackson, Mississippi
(180)	No date	POWLEDGE, FRED A.	Atlanta Journal	Atlanta, Georgia
(181)	9/19/62	RATHER, DAN	CBS News	Dallas, Texas
(182)	9/20/62	RAY, CHARLIE	WNOE	New Orleans, Louisiana
(183)	9/20/62	REESE, ANDY	United Press International	Memphis, Tennessee
(184)	9/28/62	RICHARDSON, NORMAN	Shreveport Times	Shreveport, Louisiana
(185)	9/29/62	ROACH, JACK	Charleston, South Carolina Evening Post	Charleston, South Carolina
(186)	9/28/62	ROBERTSON, VIC	WFAA-TV	Dallas, Texas
(187)	9/19/62	ROBSON, ROSCOE	Commercial Dispatch	Columbus, Mississippi
(188)	9/28/62	ROGERS, JOHN B.	Denver Post	Denver, Colorado
(189)	9/26/62	ROTHWELL, BRUCE	London Daily Mail	Washington, D. C.
(190)	9/18/62	ROTMAN, BERN	WDSU-TV	New Orleans, Louisiana
(191)	9/27/62	ROYAL, LLOYD, JR.	WQIC	Meridian, Mississippi
(192)	9/26/62	RUDD, HUGHES	CBS News	New York City New York
(193)	9/19/62	RUSH, JOHANN	CBS	Jackson, Mississippi
(194)	9/27/62	RYAN, BILL	NBC News	New York City New York
(195)	9/28/62	SANDERSON, GEORGE	KRLD-TV	Dallas, Texas
(196)	9/18/62	SAVELL, VAN H.	Associated Press	Jackson, Mississippi
(197)	9/27/62	SAVITT, SAMUEL	NBC News	Chicago, Illinois
(198)	9/28/62	SAXTON, BOB	WRAG Radio	Carrollton, Alabama
(199)	9/24/62	SCHEFFLER, PHILIP	CBS News	New York City New York
(200)	No date	SCHUBRING, VERN J.	CBS	Jackson, Mississippi

(201)	9/18/62	SCHULKE, FLIP	Life	Miami, Florida
(202)	No date	SCHWARTZ, HERB	CBS News	New York City, New York
(203)	No date	SEGERBERG, OSBORN	United Press International Movetone	New York City, New York
(204)	9/18/62	SHEARIN, JIM	Commercial Appeal	Memphis, Tennessee
(205)	9/27/62	SHEARS, DAVID	London Daily Telegram	Washington, D. C.
(206)	No date	SHIPP, BILL	Atlanta Constitution	Atlanta, Georgia
(207)	9/20/62	SHOEMAKER, W. C.	Jackson Daily News	Jackson, Mississippi
(208)	9/26/62	SHOOK, EDGAR	Time Magazine	Atlanta, Georgia
(209)	9/27/62	SIEG, CHARLES	NBC News	New York City New York
(210)	No date	SILVER, LOUIS	Commercial Appeal	Memphis, Tennessee
(211)	No date	SILVER, WILLIAM	NBC	Jackson, Mississippi
(212)	9/29/62	SILVERMAN	NBC News	New York City New York
(213)	9/19/62	SIMPSON, BILL	Daily Corinthian	Corinth, Mississippi
(214)	No date	SIMS, PATRICK M.	Sims Assoc.	Dallas, Texas
(215)	9/19/62	SITTON, CLAUDE	New York Times	Atlanta, Georgia
(216)	No date	SKELTON, B. J.	Press Register	Clarksdale, Mississippi
(217)	No date	SLADE, PAUL	Paris ?	Paris, France
(218)	9/25/62	SLAPPEY, STERLING	US News and World Rep.	Washington, D. C.
(219)	9/28/62	SLATER, BILL	WDSU-TV	New Orleans, Louisiana
(220)	9/20/62	SMITH, DAVENPORT	WBRC	Birmingham, Alabama
(221)	9/28/62	SMITH, EDDIE	WMOX	Meridian, Mississippi
(222)	9/26/62	SMITH, GARY B.	WDKK Radio	Meridian, Mississippi
(223)	9/20/62	SMITH, MIKE	Life	Miami, Florida
(224)	9/28/62	SMITH, REGGIE	Westinghouse Broadcasting	Cleveland, Ohio
(225)	9/28/62	SPEAKER, FNU	Bolivar?	Cleveland, Mississippi
(226)	9/29/62	STALLWORTH, JERRY	WCOC	Meridian, Mississippi
(227)	9/20/62 9/28/62	STANTON, ELVIN L.	WSGA (or WSGN Radio)	Birmingham, Alabama
(228)	9/27/62	STARNES, RICHARD	Scripps Howard	New York City, New York
(229)	9/26/62	STEINER, EARL JOE	CBS TV News Department	Washington, D. C.
(230)	9/29/62	STERN, JOSEPH	Baltimore Sun	Chevy Chase, Maryland
(231)	9/24/62	STEVENS, CHARLOTTE	WMPS	Memphis, Tennessee

(232)	9/19/62	STEVENS, DON	WMPS	Memphis, Tennessee
(233)	9/28/62	STEWART, JACK	WMOX	Meridian, Mississippi
(234)	No date	STOCK, SHELDON	NBC	Miami, Florida
(235)	No date	STOGNER, CHARLES	WDAM-TV	Hattiesburg, Mississippi
(236)	9/18/62	STREET, BILL	Commercial Appeal	Memphis, Tennessee
(237)	9/28/62	SUTTON, BOB	KGVW	Shreveport, Louisiana
(238)	No date	TALLEY, JAMES M.	Nashville Tennessean	Nashville, Tennessee
(239)	9/27/62	TATE, HARVEY	WMPS	Memphis, Tennessee
(240)	9/20/62 9/25/62	TAYLOR, BOBBY	WNAU Radio	New Albany, Mississippi
(241)	9/20/62	TELES, HENRY	WWL-TV	New Orleans, Louisiana
(242)	9/28/62	THOMAS, ALEX	Huntsville Times	Huntsville, Alabama
(243)	9/20/62	THORNELL, JACK	Daily News	Jackson, Mississippi
(244)	9/19/62	TOLHURST, JAMES H.	WDSU-TV	New Orleans, Louisiana
(245)	9/28/62	TOWNLEY, RICHARD	KSLA-TV	Shreveport, Louisiana
(246)	9/27/62	TRIKOSKO, MARION	US News and World Rep.	Washington, D. C.
(247)	9/27/62	TUCK, CECIL	Radio	Houston, Texas
(248)	9/26/62	TUCKER, CARNELL	WHNY Radio	McComb, Mississippi
(249)	9/28/62	TURNER, ED	KWTV Ch. 9	Oklahoma City, Okla.
(250)	9/28/62	TUTTLE, RICK	Miami Herald	Tallahassee, Florida
(251)	9/28/62	UNDERWOOD, DON	Life	Miami, Florida
(252)	9/26/62	VALERIANI. RICHARD G.	NBC News	New York City New York
(253)	9/20/62	WADE, MIKE	Daily Sentinal	Nashville, Tennessee
(254)	9/20/62	WALKER, B. F.	WBRC	Birmingham, Alabama
(255)	9/27/62	WALLICK, WALTE	Radio & TV	London
(256)	9/28/62	WARD, BOB	Huntsville Times	Huntsville, Alabama
(257)	9/28/62	WARD, FRED	Black Star Pub. Co.	New York City New York
(258)	9/28/62	WARD, REGGIE, JR.	KTBS-TV	Shreveport, Louisiana
(259)	9/20/62	WARNER, CARL	Movietonews	Miami, Florida
(260)	9/19/62	WATERS, FRED	Associated Press	St. Louis, Missouri
(261)	No date	WEATHERBY, W. J.	Manchester Guardian	Manchester ?
(262)	9/26/62	WEEMS, A. G.	WDKK Radio	Meridian, Mississippi

(263)	9/28/62	WELLS, BOB	WKDL Radio	Clarksdale Mississipp
(264)	9/21/62	WHALEY, CHARLES	The Courier Journal	Louisville Kentucky
(265)	9/20/62	WHITE, JOHNNY	WNAU Radio	New Albany Mississipp
(266)	9/28/62	WHITE, PAT J.	KTBS-TV	Shreveport Louisiana
(267)	9/28/62	WHITEFORD, CHARLES	Baltimore Sun	Baltimore, Maryland
(268)	9/27/62	WHITELEY, BOB	Radio	Memphis, Tennessee
(269)	9/20/62	WILBOURNE, BILL	Radio WDAL	Meridian, Mississipp
(270)	9/28/62	WILLIAMS, BOB	Commercial Appeal	Memphis, Tennessee
(271)	No date	WILLIAMS, DON	Ft. Worth Star Telegram	Ft. Worth, Texas
(272)	9/28/62	WROTEN, KEITH	WNAU Radio	New Albany Mississipp
(273)	9/28/62	YARBROUGH, TOM	St. Louis Post-Dispatch	St. Louis, Missouri
(274)	9/27/62	YODER, GORDON	Telenews	Dallas, Texas
(275)	9/27/62	YODER, IRENE	Telenews	Dallas, Texas
(276)	No date	YOUNG, PAUL D.	KFDA-TV	Amarillo, Texas

NOTES

Introduction

1. For more information about the theory of interposition see James J. Kilpatrick, *The Southern Case for School Segregation* (New York, Questia, 1962) and William P. Huswit, *James J. Kilpatrick: Salesman for Segregation* (Chapel Hill: University of North Carolina Press, 2013).

2. *Brown v. Board of Education of Topeka*, 347 U.S. 483 (1954). The unanimous (9–0) decision stated "separate educational facilities are inherently unequal." The justices declared racial segregation a violation of the 14th Amendment.

3. Jean Lagrance, "To a Fallen Colleague," *The Washington Post*, 3 October 1962.

4. Lagrance.

5. *Brown v. Board of Education of Topeka*, 349 U.S. 294 (1955).

6. Dr. Jerry T. Francisco, FBI interview, Oct. 1, 1962, records of the U.S. Marshals Service, Record Group 527, file number 157-147, National Archives, Southeast Region, Monroe, Ga., and Autopsy Reports, FBI James Meredith Freedom of Information File, Record Group 157-401-582 and 157-401-607.

7. John Herbers, "The Reporter in the Deep South, *Nieman Reports* 56, no. 2 (April 1962): 3.

8. Claude Sitton, interviewer unknown, transcript provided Baylor University Center for Oral History, *National Symposium on the Media and the Civil Rights Movement*, University of Mississippi, April 3, 1987, Archives and Special Collections, J.D. Williams Library, University of Mississippi.

9. J.D. Williams, An address before The Commonwealth Club of California, February 21, 1963, Russell Barrett Collection, Archives and Special collections, J.D. Williams Library, University of Mississippi.

10. Williams.

11. Williams.

12. John Griffin Jones, *Mississippi Writers Talking: Interviews with Eudora Welty, Shelby Foote, Elizabeth Spencer, Barry Hannah, Beth Henley* (Jackson, University Press of Mississippi, 1982), 56.

13. Ithiel de Sola and Irwin Shulman, "Newsmen's fantasies, audiences, and newswriting," *Public Opinion Quarterly* 23 (summer 1959) 145:58.

14. Thomas J. Sugrue, *Sweet Land of Liberty: The Forgotten Struggle for Civil Rights in the North* (New York: Random House, 2008).

15. Richard Starnes, Scripps Howard Newspaper Alliance, Sept. 30, 1962, Western Union Telegram Collection, Archives and Special Collections, J.D. Williams Library, University of Mississippi.

16. Bern Rotman, *Newsday*, Western Union Telegram Collection, Archives and Special Collections, J.D. Williams Library, University of Mississippi, Oxford, Miss., Sept. 27, 1962.

17. Mark Levy, "Watching TV News as Para-Social Interaction," *Journal of Broadcasting* 23, no.1 (1979): 69-80.

18. Dan Rather, *Without Fear and With Courage: Honoring the Reporters who covered the Ole Miss Integration Crisis*, School of Journalism & New Media, University of Mississippi, April 14, 2010.

19. Hoke Norris, *Chicago Sun-Times*, September 30, 1962, Western Union Telegram collection, Archives and Special Collections, J.D. Williams Library, University of Mississippi, and Araminta Stone Johnston, *And One Was a Priest* (Jackson: University Press of Mississippi, 2011)

Paul Guihard

20. Jean Lagrance, "To a Fallen Colleague," *The Washington Post*, October 3, 1962.

21. Lagrance, "To a Fallen Colleague."

22. Frequently cited theories place the blame on a rough U.S. marshal, the FBI, a sailor from the Millington Naval Air Station or a kitchen worker. None of these theories resulted in the identification of a shooter: "Sheriff Asks Feds Check Own Guns," The (*Jackson, Miss.) Daily News*, 16 October 1962; Bill E. Burk, "Reporter's Death Still a Mystery," *The (Knoxville, Tenn.) News-Sentinel*, 16 October 1962; Dickson Preston, "Boy May have Seen the Killing at Ole Miss," *Memphis (Tenn.) Press Scimitar*, 18 October 1962; Mississippi State Sovereignty Commission, "Lafayette County; Oxford, Mississippi; pertaining to the shooting of Ray Gunter, Oxford, Mississippi, and Paul Guirhard (sic) newsman," Mississippi Sovereignty Commission, Mississippi Department of Archives and History, SCR ID 2-19-20.

23. Evan Thomas, *Robert Kennedy: His Life* (New York: Simon & Shuster, 2000), p. 203.

24. Alain Guihard, interview with author, St. Malo, France, March 14, 2016.

25. Dickson Preston, "Boy May Have Seen the Killing at Ole Miss," *Memphis (Tenn.) Press Scimitar*, 13 October 1962.

26. "Slaying Suspect may be prisoner," *Birmingham News*, October 15, 1962.

27. "Sheriff Asks Feds Check Own Guns."

28. Felix Bolo, AFP supervisor/manager, letter to author William Doyle, December 5, 1999, William Doyle Collection, Archives and Special Collections, John D. Williams Library, University of Mississippi. Bolo says Schulman was a stringer. However, Schulman's obituary in *New York Times* says Schulman was head of photo operations: "Sammy Schulman Dead; Was Press Photographer," *New York Times*, 22 August 1980.

29. "Sammy Schulman Dead."

30. Sammy Schulman, *Where's Sammy?* (New York: Random House, 1943).

31. Schulman, *Where's Sammy?*

32. "Kennedy is Dismayed by Killing of French Newsman During Riots," *The New York Times*, 5 October 1962.

33. George B. Leonard, T. George Harris, and Christopher S. Wren, "How a Secret Deal Prevented a Massacre at Ole Miss," *Look*, December 31, 1962; Sterling Slappey and Marion S. Trikosko, "I Saw It Happen in Oxford," *U.S. News & World Report*, October 15, 1962.

34. Slappey and Triosko, p. 23.

35. Slappey and Triosko, p. 24.

36. Slappey and Triosko, p. 24.

37. James Silver, *Mississippi: The Closed Society* (New York: Harcourt, Brace & World, 1964).

38. President's Office Files, September 30, 1962, John F. Kennedy Library.

39. George B. Leonard, T. George Harris, and Christopher S. Wren, "How a Secret Deal Prevented a Massacre," and Slappey and Triosko, "I Saw It Happen in Oxford."

40. "Ole Miss Gets U.S. list of Students Tied to Riot," *Washington Post*, 11 October 1962.

41. Carroll Kirkpatrick, "President in Talk to Nation Urges Law and Order," *The Washington Post*, 1 October 1962.

42. Roberts and Klibanoff, *The Race Beat: The Press, the Civil Rights Struggle, and the Awakening of a Nation.* (New York: Knopf, 2006), 294.

43. Bill E. Burk, "Reporter's Death Still a Mystery," *The (Knoxville, Tenn.) News-Sentinel*, 12 October 1962.

44. Leonard, Harris and Wren, "How a Secret Deal Prevented a Massacre," and Slappey and Triosko, "I Saw It Happen in Oxford."

45. Leonard, Harris and Wren, "How a Secret Deal Prevented a Massacre," and Slappey and Triosko, "I Saw It Happen in Oxford."

46. SA Robin O. Cotton, FBI report, Oct. 8, 1962, Records of the U.S. Marshals Service, Record Group 527, File Number 157-147, National Archives, Southeast Region, Monroe, Ga.

47. Guihard, interview.

48. Guihard, interview.

49. "JFK Shocked by Slaying of Reporter," *The Washington Post*, 2 October 1962; "Kennedy is Dismayed by Killing of French Newsman During Riots," *The New York Times*, 5 October 1962.

50. "The High Price of News," *London (England) Daily Sketch*, 2 October 1962.

51. Rev. Michel Leutellier, interview by author, St. Malo, France, March 14, 2016.

52. Leutellier.

53. Leutellier.

54. Flip Schulke, interview by Rebecca Nappi, transcript, *Civil Rights Oral History Interviews*, Washington State University and Joe Holley, "Flip Schulke, 77; Photographer Acclaimed For Coverage of Civil Rights Movement, *Washington Post*, May 17, 2008.

55. Robert S. Bird, "A Night to Remember," *New York Herald-Tribune*, 14 October 1962.

56. Flip Schulke, interview by Rebecca Nappi.

57. Flip Schulke, *Witness to Our Times: My life as a Photojournalist*, (Chicago: Cricket Books, 2003): 24.

58. "Though the heavens fall," *Time*, 12 October 1962.

59. Thomas, *Robert Kennedy: His Life*.

60. Michael Dorman, *We Shall Overcome: A Reporter's Eyewitness Account of the Year of Racial Strife and Triumph* (New York: Delacote Press, 1964): 77.

61. SA Robin O. Cotton, FBI report, Oct. 8, 1962, Records of the U.S. Marshals Service, Record Group 527, File Number 157-147, National Archives, Southeast Region, Monroe, Ga.

62. James Meredith, interview by Jared Boyd and Logan Kirkland, Jackson, Miss, February 29, 2016.

63. "The Sound and the Fury," *Newsweek*, October 15, 1962.

64. Hugh Calvin Murray, FBI interview, Oct. 8, 1962, Records of the U.S. Marshals Service, Record Group 527, File Number 157-147, National Archives, Southeast Region, Monroe, Ga.

65. Murray.

66. Johann W. Rush, FBI interview, Nov. 6, 1962, Records of the U.S. Marshals Service, Record Group 527, File Number 157-221, National Archives, Southeast Region, Monroe, Ga.

67. Murray, FBI interview.

68. Tom Brown, transcript, Oct. 8, 1962, Records of the U.S. Marshals Service, Record Group 527, No file number, National Archives, Southeast Region, Monroe, Ga.

69. Brown.

70. Murray, FBI interview.

71. Murray.

72. Brown, transcript.

73. Cort Best, FBI interview, Oct. 30, 1962, Records of the U.S. Marshals Service, Record Group 527, File Number 157-118, National Archives, Southeast Region, Monroe, Ga., File Number 11-5-62.

74. R. J. Bonds, FBI interview, Oct. 25, 1962, Records of the U.S. Marshals Service, Record Group 527, File Number 157-147, National Archives, Southeast Region, Monroe, Ga.

The YMCA building is now the location of the Croft Institute for International Studies. The YMCA building served as a recreation center on campus. It is located near Bryant Hall, the former Fine Arts building, on the north side of the green space in front of the Lyceum.

75. Brown, transcript.

76. Rush, FBI interview, Brown transcript and author interview with Brown, July 18, 2008.

77. Brown, transcript.

78. Donald Lee Dugger, FBI interview, Oct. 6, 1962, Records of the U.S. Marshals Service, Record Group 527, File Number 157-147, National Archives, Southeast Region, Monroe, Ga.

79. Brown, transcript.

80. Sutherland, FBI report.

81. Elliott, transcript.

82. Dr. Jerry T. Francisco, FBI interview, Oct. 1, 1962, Records of the U.S. Marshals Service, Record Group 527, file number 157-147. National Archives, Southeast Region, and Autopsy Reports, FBI James Meredith Freedom of Information File, Record Group 157-401-582 and 157-401-607.

83. Sidna Brower Mitchell, telephone interview with author, February 13, 2009.

84. G. H. McLarty, FBI interview, Oct. 3, 1962, Records of the U.S. Marshals Service, Record Group 527, File Number 157-147, National Archives, Southeast Region, Monroe, Ga.

85. Francisco, FBI interview.

86. Anthony Harrigan, telegram to Doug Donahue, *The Charleston (S.C.) News & Courier*, Western Union Telegram Collection, Archives and Special Collections, J.D. Williams Library, University of Mississippi, Oxford, Miss.

87. Richard Starnes, telegram begins: "Madness swept the Ole Miss campus tonight," Scripps Howard Newspaper Alliance, Western Union Telegram Collection, Archives and Special Collections, J.D. Williams Library, University of Mississippi, Oxford, Miss.

88. Starnes.

89. John F. Kennedy telegram to M. Jean Martin, president and general manager Agence France-Presse, President's Office Files, October 1, 1962, John F. Kennedy Presidential Library, Boston, Mass.

90. Guihard, interview.

91. Guihard, correspondence to author, June 29, 2008.

92. Guihard, correspondence.

93. Jean Lagrance, "To a Fallen Colleague," *Washington Post*, 3 October 1962: translated by Ellen Everett, University of Mississippi, Oxford, Miss.

94. "Kennedy is Dismayed by Killing of French Newsman During Riots."

95. Felix Bolo letter to William Doyle.

96. Guihard, interview.

97. Last Report from Dead Newsman, *The Washington Post*, 2 October 1962.

98. Karl Fleming, "Birth of the Movement: World War II through the 1950s," transcript, *National Symposium on the Media and the Civil Rights Movement*, April 3-5, 1987, Archives and Special Collections, J.D. Williams Library, University of Mississippi.

Claude Sitton

99. Claude Sitton, interview by author, Oxford, Georgia, May 15, 2010.

100. Sitton, interview by author.

101. Karl Fleming, memo, Harrison Salisbury Papers, Rare Book and Manuscript Library, Columbia University, April 18, 1979.

102. Sitton, interview by Sarah Buynovsky, transcript, *Civil Rights and The Press Symposium*, S.I. Newhouse School of Public Communications, Syracuse University, April 24, 2004. http://civilrightsandthepress.syr.edu/oral_histories.html (accessed July 15, 2011).

103. Sitton, *National Symposium on the Media and the Civil Rights Movement*.

104. Sitton, interview by Sarah Buynovsky.

105. Sitton, interview by author.

106. Claude Sitton, Harrison Salisbury Papers, Rare Book and Manuscript Library, Columbia University, March 18, 1979.

107. Sitton, interview by Sarah Buynovsky.

108. Sitton, interview by author.

109. Sitton, memo, Salisbury Papers.

110. Craig Schneider, "Claude Sitton's courageous reporting influenced civil rights struggle," *The Atlanta Journal-Constitution*, 10 March 2015.

111. Sitton, interview by Sarah Buynovsky.

112. Harry Ashmore, "Covering History as It Broke: John N. Popham," *Southern Changes*, vol. 6, no. 1 (1984).

113. Claude Sitton, interviewer unknown, transcript provided Baylor University Center for Oral History, *National Symposium on the Media and the Civil Rights Movement*, April 3, 1987, Archives and Special Collections, J.D. Williams Library, University of Mississippi.

114. Claude Sitton, "Setting the Scene: The Landscape of Civil Rights & Press Coverage," *Civil Rights and the Press Symposium*, transcript, Syracuse University, April 24, 2005, http://civilrightsandthepress.syr.edu (accessed July 13, 2011).

115. Sitton, interview by Sarah Buynovsky.

116. Sitton, memo, March 18, 1979.

117. Sitton, interviewed by Sarah Buynovsky.

118. Sitton, interview by Sarah Buynovsky.

119. James Meredith, letter to author, March 15, 2017.

Karl Fleming

120. Karl Fleming, interview by Tavis Smiley, National Public Radio, July 13, 2005.

121. Karl Fleming, *Son of the Rough South* (New York: Public Affairs, 2005), 229.

122. Karl Fleming, interview by Jim Pratt, transcript provided Baylor University Center for Oral History, *National Symposium on the Media and the Civil Rights Movement*, Archives and Special Collections, J.D. Williams Library, University of Mississippi, April 3, 1987.

123. "Mississippi: The Sound and the Fury," *Newsweek*, October 15, 1962, and William Faulkner, *The Sound and the Fury* (New York: Jonathan Cape & Harrison Smith, 1929.)

124. Ted McKown, "Faulkner Talks to Reporters about Integration, Virginians, Charlotte Daily Progress," In *Conversations with William Faulkner*, ed. M. Thomas Inge (Jackson: University Press of Mississippi, 1999).

125. Mississippi: The Sound and the Fury, *Newsweek*, October 15, 1962.

126. Fleming, *Son of the Rough South*, 269.

127. Karl Fleming, interview by Leslie Jack, *Civil Rights and The Press Symposium*, 2005, S.I. Newhouse School of Public Communications, Syracuse University. Transcript available: http://civilrightsandthepress.syr.edu/oral_histories.html.

128. Karl Fleming, memo, April 13, 1979, Harrison Salisbury Papers, Rare Book and Manuscript Library, Columbia University.

129. Fleming, interview by Jim Pratt.

130. Fleming, *Son of the Rough South*, 275.

131. Harvey Tate, DOJ interview, Oct. 26, 1962, Records of the U.S. Marshals Service, Record Group 527, File number Memphis 157-147, National Archives, Southeast Region, Monroe, Ga.

132. Karl Fleming, DOJ interview, Oct. 4, 1962, Records of the U.S. Marshals Service, Record Group 527, no file number, National Archives, Southeast Region, Monroe, Ga.

133. Fleming, DOJ interview.

134. Fleming, *Son of the Rough South*, 285.

135. Fleming, *Son of the Rough South*, 289.

136. Fleming, interviewed by Jim Pratt.

137. Karl Fleming, transcript, "Killing Jim Crow: The 1964 Civil Rights Act," *Civil Rights and the Press Symposium*, S.I. Newhouse School of Public Communications, Syracuse University, April 24, 2005, Available: http://civilrightsandthepress.syr.edu.

138. Karl Fleming, transcript, "Setting the Scene: The Landscape of Civil Rights & Press Coverage," *Civil Rights and the Press Symposium*, S.I. Newhouse School of Public Communications, Syracuse University, April 24, 2005. Available: http://civilrightsandthepress.syr.edu.

Michael Dorman

139. William Faulkner, *Intruder in the Dust* (New York: Random House, 1948).

140. Joseph Blotner, ed. Selected letters of William Faulkner (New York: Random House), 1977.

141. Robert W. Hamblin, *Myself and the World: A biography of William Faulkner* (Jackson: University Press of Mississippi, 2016) 119.

142. Faulkner, *Intruder in the Dust*, 49.

143. Dorman, *We Shall Overcome*, 33.

144. Michael Dorman, "Oxford, 1962, Is Faulkner Novel Come True," *Newsday*, Long Island, New York.

145. Dorman, *We Shall Overcome*, 37.

146. Dorman.

147. *Miami Herald*, September 30, 1962, Western Union Telegram Collection, Archives and Special Collections, J.D. Williams Library, University of Mississippi.

148. Vincent Harding, Day One, Pre-production School session, transcript, Audio FMA 2-8160 3-3-1, *Eyes on the Prize: America's Civil Rights Years (1954-1965)*, Henry Hampton Collection, Film and Media Archive, Washington University of St. Louis.

149. Dorman, *We Shall Overcome*, 37.

150. Dorman, *We Shall Overcome*, 38.

151. Dean Faulkner Wells, *Every Day by the Sun: A Memoir of the Faulkners of Mississippi* (New York, Crown Publishing Group, 2008), 181.

152. William Doyle, *An American Insurrection: The Battle of Oxford, Mississippi, 1962*, (New York: Doubleday, 2001) 203.

153. Dorman, *We Shall Overcome*, 53.

154. President's Office Files, September 30, 1962, John F. Kennedy Library.

155. Dorman, *We Shall Overcome*, 108.

Dan Rather

156. Dan Rather, *Without Fear and With Courage: Honoring the Reporters who covered the Ole Miss Integration Crisis*, School of Journalism & New Media, University of Mississippi, April 14, 2010.

157. Elmo Roper, *The public's view of television and other media 1959-1964* (New York: Television Information Office, 1965): 1-2.

158. Rather, *Without Fear and With Courage.*

159. Rather.

160. Rather.

161. Rather.

162. Rather.

163. Rather.

164. Rather.

165. Dan Rather interview, Archive of American Television, 2005. Available: http://aat.fivepaths-dev.com/interviews/people/dan-rather.

166. Dan Rather, *The Camera Never Blinks* (New York: William Morrow, 1977), 72.

167. Dan Rather interview, Archive of American Television, 2005. Available: http://aat.fivepaths-dev.com/interviews/people/dan-rather.

168. Rather, *The Camera Never Blinks*, p. 74.

169. Rather, *Without Fear and With Courage.*

170. Rather, *The Camera Never Blinks*, p. 75.

171. Dan Rather, FBI Interview, Nov. 1, 1962, National Archives, Southeast Region, Monroe, Ga., Records of the U.S. Marshals Service, Record Group 527, File number, NY 157-755.

172. Rather, *The Camera Never Blinks*, p. 76.

173. Rather, *Without Fear and With Courage.*

174. Dan Rather, *Forum on Press Coverage of the American Civil Rights Movement*, John F. Kennedy Memorial Library, Boston, Mass., March 24, 1998. Available: www.cbsnews.com.stoires/1998/03/30/civilrights/main62.

175. Rather interview, Archive of American Television, 2005. Available: http://aat.fivepaths-dev.com/interviews/people/dan-rather.

176. Rather, *Without Fear and With Courage.*

Moses Newson

177. Interview with author, January 11, 2017.

178. Charles Eagles, *The Price of Defiance: James Meredith and the Integration of Ole Miss* (Chapel Hill: University of North Carolina Press, 2009) 509.

179. Interview with author.

180. Interview with author.

181. Brian Palmer, 50 Years Later: A Veteran Newsman on Covering the Civil Rights Struggle, August 26, 2013. Available: http://communitytable.parade.com/63345/brianpalmer/50-years-later-a-veteran-newsman-on-covering-the-civil-rights-struggle.

182. Interview with author.

183. Ibid.

184. Ibid.

185. Wil Haygood, "Story Of Their Lives; For Reporters on the Civil Rights Beat, The Trick Was to Cover The News, Not Be It," *Washington Post*, Nov. 26, 2006.

186. James L. Hicks, interview conducted by Blackside, Inc., November 2, 1985, for *Eyes on the Prize: America's Civil Rights Years (1954-1965)*, Henry Hampton Collection, Film and Media Archive, Washington University of St. Louis.

187. David L. Chappell, Roads to Freedom, *The Nation*, May 7, 2007.

188. Moses Newson, interview by Marshand Boone, April 24, 2004, *Civil Rights and The Press Symposium*, S.I. Newhouse School of Public Communications, Syracuse University. Transcript available: http://civilrightsandthepress.syr.edu/oral_histories.html.

189. James L. Hicks, interview conducted by Blackside, Inc.

190. "Book Examines Covering the Race Beat," National Public Radio, February 1, 2007, Transcript available: http://www.npr.org/templates/story/story.php?storyId=7115416.

191. Newson, interview by Marshand Boone.

Flip Schulke

192. Flip Schulke, interviewed by Scott Stines, transcript, Civil Rights Oral History Interviews, *Spokesman-Review*, January 30, 2001, Manuscripts, Archives and Special Collections, Washington State University.

193. Schulke.

194. Schulke.

195. Schulke.

196. Schulke.

197. Flip Schulke, *Witness to Our Times* (Chicago: Cricket Books), 2003.

198. Schulke, *Witness to Our Times*, p. 2.

199. Flip Schulke, *Connect Business*, http://connectbiz.com/2007/07/flip-schulke.

200. Schulke, *Witness to Our Times*, p. 2

201. Schulke, *Witness to Our Times*, p. 6.

202. Schulke, *Connect Business*.

203. Schulke, *Witness to Our Times*, p. xvi.

204. Schulke, *Witness to Our Times*.

205. Schulke, interviewed by Scott Stines.

Sidna Brower

206. Kay Veasey, interview by author, Memphis, Tenn., Dec. 5, 2016.

207. Veasey, interview.

208. Sidna Brower, interview by author, Washington, D.C., June 4, 2016.

209. Brower.

210. Sidna Brower, transcript, *Inside Media: James Meredith and the Integration of Ole Miss and the March Against Fear*, Newseum, Washington, D.C. June 4, 2016.

211. Brower, interview.

212. Brower, interview.

213. Brower, *Inside Media*.

214. "Dickson Preston, Girl Editor Roasts 'Ole Miss' rioters," *Memphis (Tenn.) Press-Scimitar*, 5 October 1962.

215. Stan Opotowsky, no headline, Western Union Telegram Collection, Archives & Special Collections, J.D. Williams Library, The University of Mississippi.

216. Preston, "Girl Editor."

217. Brower, *Inside Media*

218. Sidna Brower, interview by author, Feb. 13, 2009.

219. Brower.

220. Brower, interview, June 4, 2016.

221. Brower.

222. Sidna Brower, presentation, School of Journalism and New Media, University of Mississippi, October 5, 2009.

223. Federal marshals surrounded the historic Lyceum Building Sunday afternoon (photograph caption), *The Mississippian*, October 1, 1962.

224. Jan Humber, "Chancellor Issues Plea; Death, injuries from campus rioting," *The Mississippian*, October 1, 1962.

225. Wil Haygood, "A Mississippi Odyssey," *The Washington Post*, 29 September 2002.

226. George Berkin, "Ole Miss corrected an old wrong from the civil rights era," *The (Newark, N.J.) Star-Ledger*, September 26, 2002.

227. Brower, interview, June 4, 2016.

228. Bob Considine, "On the line" Hearst Headline Service, Special Collections Research Center Syracuse University, Oct. 2, 1962.

229. Sidna Brower Mitchell Collection, Archives and Special Collections, J.D. Williams Library, University of Mississippi.

230. Brower.

231. Wil Haygood, "A Mississippi Odyssey," *The Washington Post*, 29 September 2002.

232. Brower, interview, June 4, 2016.

233. Brower.

234. Brower.

235. James Silver, *Mississippi: The Closed Society* (New York: Harcourt, Brace & World, 1964).

236. Brower, interview, June 4, 2016.

237. Wil Haygood, "A Mississippi Odyssey."

238. Brower, interview, June 4, 2016.

239. Berkin, Ole Miss corrects an old wrong from the civil rights era."

240. Mississippi Student Group Denounces Campus Editor, *The New York Times*, 29 November 1962.

241. Wil Haygood, "A Mississippi Odyssey."

242. Thomas Buckley, Mississippi U Fears effect of Court's Reinstatement of Expelled Student," *The New York Times*, 4 December 1962.

243. Buckley.

244. Brower presentation.

245. Dwight Lewis, "Vindicated where she once was told not to speak for peace," *The (Nashville) Tennessean*, 3 October 1962.

246. Letter to student senate, Sidna Brower Collection, Archives and Special Collections, J.D. Williams Library, University of Mississippi.

247. Letter to student senate, Sidna Brower Collection, Archives and Special Collections, J.D. Williams Library, University of Mississippi.

248. Brower, *Inside Media.*

249. Brower, *Inside Media.*

250 Audrey Davie, Ole Miss undoes 1962 censure," *The Bernardsville News*, 3 October 1962.

251. Elaine Pugh, "Integration-era editor of UM newspaper donates letters, other memorabilia," *The Oxford Eagle*, August 19, 2011.

252. Brower presentation.

253. William Street, "Ole Miss Editor, Storm Hub, Does 'What I Think Is Right,'" *The Guild Reporter*, December 28, 1962.

254. Lewis, "Vindicated"

255. Berkin, Ole Miss corrects an old wrong from the civil rights era."

256. Haygood, "A Mississippi Odyssey."

257. Brower, interview, June 4, 2016.

258. Sidna Brower, James Meredith File, Mississippi State Sovereignty Commission, SCR 1-67-3-31-1-1-1, 1-67-3-78-1-1-1, 1-67-4-16-1-1-1, 1-67-4-22-1-1-1, Mississippi Department of Archives and History.

259. Ada Gilkey, Ole Miss has Student Editor from Memphis, *Memphis (Tenn.) Press-Scimitar*, 3 October 1962.

260. Brower, interview, June 4, 2016.

261. Brower.

262. Sidna Brower Mitchell Collection.

263. Brower, interview, February 13, 2009.

Fred Powledge

264. Fred Powledge, telephone interview with author, October 19, 2016.

265. "The Mass Movement, 1960-64 (Part 2)," *National Symposium on the Media and the Civil Rights Movement April 3-5, 1987*, transcript, Archives and Special collections, J.D. Williams Library, University of Mississippi.

266. Fred Powledge, interviewer not identified, transcript provided Baylor University Center for Oral History, *National Symposium on the Media and the Civil Rights Movement*, Archives and Special Collections, J.D. Williams Library, University of Mississippi, April 3, 1987.

267. Powledge.

268. Charles Moore, telephone interview with author, November 11, 2008.

269. Fred Powledge, DOJ transcript, no date, National Archives, Southeast Region, Monroe, Ga., Records of the U.S. Marshals Service, Record Group 527, no file number.

270. Powledge, interview with author.

271. Gene Sherman, Los Angeles Times, September 30, 1962, Western Union Telegram collection, Archives and Special Collections, J.D. Williams Library, University of Mississippi.

272. Powledge, DOJ transcript.

273. James McShane, transcript, Records of the U.S. Marshals Service, Record Group 527, National Archives, Southeast Region, Monroe, Ga.

274. McShane.

275. McShane.

276. McShane.

277. Fred Powledge, interview.

278. Associated Press, Marshal Describes Attack by Students, The *(Jackson, Miss.) Daily News*, October 8, 1962.

279. "Though the heavens fall," *Time*, October 12, 1962, 20.

280. Powledge, interview.

281. Powledge, DOJ transcript.

282. Richard Russell, "Memories from Ole Miss: Barnett, reporters to blame." *The (Jackson, Miss.) Clarion-Ledger*, September 28, 2012. http://www.clarionledger.com/article/20120930/OPINION03/309300020/ (September 30, 2012).

283. Molly Yates, "Remembering the Riots: First Hand Accounts," *The Daily Mississippian*, The University of Mississippi, September 26, 2012, 1.

284. Michael Lollar, "Violence Helped Forge New Ole Miss, *The (Memphis, Tenn.) Commercial Appeal*, October 1, 2012, sec A., p. 1.

285. Powledge, interview.

286. Powledge, DOJ transcript.

287. Powledge, interview.

288. Powledge.

289. Powledge, DOJ transcript.

290. Powledge.

291. Powledge.

292. Powledge, interview.

293. Powledge, Baylor University Center for Oral History.

294. Powledge, interview.

295. "The Mass Movement, 1960-64 (Part 2)."

Gordon Yoder

296. UPI, Rocks Thrown at Reporters in Pine Bluff, *Sarasota (Florida) Journal*, 25 August 1959, and Gordon Yoder, obituary, *The Dallas Morning News*, 16 October 2004.

297. Gordon Yoder, obituary, *The Dallas Morning News*, 16 October 2004.

298. Gordon Yoder, DOJ transcript, no date, National Archives, Southeast Region, Monroe, Ga., Records of the U.S. Marshals Service, Record Group 527, no file number.

299. Gene Sherman, "Raging Students Shout Their Anger as Tear Gas Makes Them Retreat," *Los Angeles Times*, October 1, 1962.

300. Yoder, obituary.

301. Sherman, "Raging Students Shout Their Anger."

302. "With the besieged marshals as the wild mob attacks," *Life*, October 12, 1962.

303. Irene Yoder, DOJ transcript, no date, National Archives, Southeast Region, Monroe, Ga., Records of the U.S. Marshals Service, Record Group 527, no file number.

304. Yoder, DOJ transcript.

305. Yoder.

306. G. Michael Lala, FBI Interview, Nov. 1, 1962, National Archives, Southeast Region, Monroe, Ga., Records of the U.S. Marshals Service, Record Group 527. File number, NO 157-221.

307. Yoder, DOJ transcript.

308. Yoder.

309. Yoder.

310. Yoder.

311. Irene Yoder, DOJ transcript.

312. Robert Massie, "What Next in Mississippi," *Saturday Evening Post*, November 10, 1962.

313. Yoder, DOJ transcript.

314. Yoder.

315. Michael Dorman, FBI Interview, Nov. 20, 1962, National Archives, Southeast Region, Monroe, Ga., Records of the U.S. Marshals Service, Record Group 527. File number 157-755.

316. Harold P. Kluehe, FBI Interview, Nov. 1, 1962, National Archives, Southeast Region, Monroe, Ga., Records of the U.S. Marshals Service, Record Group 527. File number 157-147.

Richard Valeriani

317. Richard Valeriani, FBI Interview, Oct. 18, 1962, National Archives, Southeast Region, Monroe, Ga., Records of the U.S. Marshals Service, Record Group 527. File number, Miami 157-700.

318. Richard Valeriani, interview with author, November 30, 2011.

319. Richard Valeriani, interview with author, November 17, 2008.

320. Valeriani, interview with author, November 30, 2011.

321. Valeriani, FBI Interview.

322. Valeriani, interview, November 30, 2011.

323. Valeriani, interview, November 17, 2008.

324. William Gordon, FBI Interview, Nov. 1 & 2, 1962, National Archives, Southeast Region, Monroe, Ga., Records of the U.S. Marshals Service, Record Group 527, File number, NK 157-935.

325. Valeriani, Interview, November 17, 2008.

326. "The Political Movement 1965-67," transcript, *National Symposium on the Media and the Civil Rights Movement* (April 3-5, 1987), Archives and Special Collections, J.D. Williams Library, University of Mississippi.

327. Richard Valeriani, interview by Mary Morin, April 24, 2004, *Civil Rights and The Press Symposium*, S.I. Newhouse School of Public Communications, Syracuse University. Transcript available: http://civilrightsandthepress.syr.edu/oral_histories. html. Accessed July 15, 2011.

328. Valeriani, interview by Mary Morin.

329. Richard Valeriani, interview by Blackside, Inc. on December 10, 1985, for Eyes on the Prize: America's Civil Rights Years (1954-1965). Henry Hampton Collection, Film and Media Archive, Washington University of St. Louis.

330. Valeriani, interview by Blackside, Inc.

331. "Killing Jim Crow: The 1964 Civil Rights Act," *Civil Rights and the Press Symposium*, Syracuse University, April 24, 2005. http://civilrightsandthepress.syr.edu/ Accessed July 13, 20011.

332. "The Political Movement 1965-67," *National Symposium on the Media and the Civil Rights Movement (April 3-5, 1987)*, Archives and Special Collections, J.D. Williams Library, University of Mississippi.

333. "Killing Jim Crow: The 1964 Civil Rights Act."

334. Valeriani, interview by Morin.

Dorothy Gilliam

335. Gilliam, email to author, Feb. 13, 2012

336. Dorothy Gilliam, transcript, "Setting the Scene: The Landscape of Civil Rights & Press Coverage," *Civil Rights and the Press Symposium*, Syracuse University, April 24, 2005, Available: http://civilrightsandthepress.syr.edu (July 13, 2011).

337. Dorothy Gilliam, interview by Donita M. Moorhus, June 9, 1994, transcript, *Washington Press Club Foundation*, Available: http://beta.wpcf.org/oralhistory/gillint.html.

338. Dorothy Gilliam, interview by Juan Williams, transcript provided Baylor University Center for Oral History, *National Symposium on the Media and the Civil Rights Movement*, Archives and Special Collections, J.D. Williams Library, University of Mississippi, April 3, 1987, and Dorothy Gilliam, "Setting the Scene."

339. Gilliam, interview by Donita M. Moorhus.

340. Dorothy Gilliam, interview by Sicilia Durazo, transcript, April 24, 2004, *Civil Rights and The Press Symposium*, S.I. Newhouse School of Public Communications, Syracuse University, Available: http://civilrightsandthepress.syr.edu/oral_histories.html.

341. Gilliam, interview by Juan Williams.

342. Gilliam, email to author.

343. Effie Burt, audience member, "Panel Discussion With People Who Were On Campus Sept. 30-Oct.1, 1962 during James Meredith Enrollment," *50 Years of*

Integration: Opening the Closed Society, University of Mississippi, September 26, 2012.

344. Effie Burt, interview by author, Oxford, Mississippi, August 13, 2016.

345. Gilliam, interview by Durazo.

346. Gilliam, interview.

347. Gilliam, "Setting the Scene."

348. Gilliam, interview by Durazo.

349. Ernest Withers, interview by Marshand Boone, transcript, April 24, 2004, *Civil Rights and The Press Symposium*, S.I. Newhouse School of Public Communications Syracuse University, Available: http://civilrightsandthepress.syr.edu/oral_histories.html.

350. Sidney L. Smith, "Getting There, Being There, Working There: The Impact of Race Upon Civil Rights Reporting in the Deep South (1955-1965)," (master's thesis, University of Mississippi, 1992).

351. Gilliam, interview by Durazo.

352. Gilliam.

353. Dorothy Gilliam, transcript, "Birth of the Movement: World War II through the 1950s," *National Symposium on the Media and the Civil Rights Movement*, Archives and Special Collections, J.D. Williams Library, University of Mississippi, April 3-5, 1987.

354. Gilliam, "Birth of the Movement."

355. Gilliam.

356. Gilliam, interview by Moorhus.

357. Gene Roberts and Hank Klibanoff, *The Race Beat* (New York: Knopf, 2006), 55.

358. Dorothy Gilliam, Civil Rights and the Press Symposium, *Setting the Scene: The Landscape of Civil Rights & Press Coverage*, Tape One, Syracuse University, April 24, 2005, Available: http://civilrightsandthepress.syr.edu/

359. Gilliam, "Birth of the Movement."

360. Smith, "Getting There, being There, Working There."

361. Turner Catledge, *My Life and the Times* (New York: Harper and Row, 1971), 218.

362. United States. Kerner Commission, Report of the National Advisory Commission on Civil Disorders (Washington: U.S. Government Printing Office, 1968).

363. Gilliam, interview by Durazo.

364. Gilliam.

Neal Gregory

365. Neal Gregory, "Withering Fire From Pulpits Rakes Mississippi's Defiance," *The (Memphis) Commercial Appeal*, 8 October 1962.

366. Neal Gregory, interview by author, Oxford, Mississippi, July 22, 1016.

367. Gregory.

368. Gregory.

369. Gregory.

370. Neal Gregory, "1,200 Students Swapping Crisis for Grid Junket," *The (Memphis) Commercial Appeal*, 6 October1962.

371. Neal Gregory, "Professors Rally To Marshals' Side And Urge Inquiry," *The (Memphis, Tenn.) Commercial Appeal*, 4 October 1962.

372. Gregory, "Professors Rally To Marshals' Side And Urge Inquiry."

373. Neal Gregory, "Walker is Free on $50,000 bail," *The (Memphis, Tenn.) Commercial Appeal*, 7 October 1962.

Conclusion

374. Duncan Gray, DOJ interview, no date, Records of the U.S. Marshals Service, Record Group 527, no file number, National Archives, Southeast Region, Monroe, Georgia.

375. Gray.

376. Robert Hamblin, *William Faulkner And Evans Harrington: A Study In Influence*, William Faulkner Conference, University of Mississippi, July 20, 2016.

377. Gray, DOJ interview.

378. Gray, DOJ interview.

379. Araminta Stone Johnston, *And One was a Priest: The Life and Times of Duncan M. Gray Jr.*, (Jackson: University Press of Mississippi), 2001, p. 21

380. Johnston, *And One Was a Priest*, p. 35.

381. John D. Harris, Hearst Headline Service, West Union Telegram Collection, Archives and Special Collections, J.D. Williams Library, University of Mississippi.

382. Hoke Norris, *Chicago Sun-Times*, September 30, 1962. Western Union Telegram Collection, Archives and Special Collections, J.D. Williams Library, University of Mississippi, Oxford, Miss.

383. Hoke Norris, *Chicago Sun-Times*.

384. Hank Klibanoff, Paul Guihard Memorial Bench Dedication, University of Mississippi, April 17, 2009.

385. Jerry Mitchell, *Without Fear and With Courage: Honoring the Reporters who covered the Ole Miss Integration Crisis*, School of Journalism & New Media, University of Mississippi, April 14, 2010.

386. Dan Rather, *Without Fear and With Courage: Honoring the Reporters who covered the Ole Miss Integration Crisis*, School of Journalism & New Media, University of Mississippi, April 14, 2010.

387. Anthony Feinstein, "The psychological hazards of war," *Neiman Reports* 58, no. 2 (Summer 2004): 76.

388. Karl Fleming, "*National Symposium on the Media and the Civil Rights Movement,* transcript provided Baylor University Center for Oral History, Archives and Special Collections, J.D. Williams Library, University of Mississippi, 3-5 April 1987.

389. Alain Guihard, interview by author, St. Malo, France, March 14, 2016.

390. Robert Wright Hooker, *Race and the News Media in Mississippi,* 1962-1964 (master's thesis, Vanderbilt University, 1971), p. 265; Susan Weill, *In a Madhouse's Din: Civil Rights Coverage by Mississippi's Daily Press, 1948-1968* (Westport, Conn.: Praeger, 2002); Gene Roberts and Hank Klibanoff, *The Race Beat: The Press, the Civil Rights Struggle, and the Awakening of a Nation.* (New York: Knopf, 2006).

391. James Silver, *Mississippi: The Closed Society* (New York: Harcourt, Brace & World, 1964).

392. Commission on the Freedom of the Press (Hutchins Commission), *A Free and Responsible Press* (Chicago: The University of Chicago Press, 1947).

393. Weill, *In a Madhouse's Din,* p. 106-113.

394. Hooker, *Race and the News Media in Mississippi,* p. 265.

395. Bill Minor, telephone interview with author, June 27, 2002.

396. Kathy Lally, "A journey from racism to reason: The Clarion-Ledger of Jackson, Miss.," *The Baltimore Sun Journal,* 5 January 1997.

397. "A Regional Report: Newspapers of the South," *Columbia Journalism Review* (Summer 1967): 26-35.

398. Roberts and Klibanoff, *The Race Beat,* p. 272.

399. Michael Patronik. "Newspaper Coverage of the Desegregation of Southern Universities" (master's thesis, University of Mississippi, 2011).

400. Patronik.

401. *Eyes on the Prize I*, School audio, Day One, transcript, Henry Hampton Collection, Film & Media Archive, Washington University at St. Louis.

402. Lally, "A journey from racism to reason."

403. Lally, "A journey from racism to reason."

404. Kathleen Woodruff Wickham, *The Role of the Clarion-Ledger in the adoption of the 1982 Education Reform Act* (Lewiston, N.Y.: The Edwin Mellen Press, 2007).

405. Hodding Carter III, interview by Courtney Brennan, S.I. Newhouse School of Public Communications, Syracuse University, http://knightpoliticalreporting.syr.edu/wp content/uploads/2012/05/hodding_carter_oral_essay.pdf.

406. Hodding Carter III, interview conducted by Blackside, Inc., October 30, 1985, Eyes on the Prize: America's Civil Rights Years (1954-1965), Henry Hampton Collection, Film and Media Archive, Washington University of St. Louis, Available http://digital.wustl.edu/eyesontheprize/

407. Hodding Carter, transcript, Civil Rights and the Press Symposium, Syracuse University, April 24, 2004.

408. Hodding Carter, interview by Jack Carter, no date, Silver Em Collection, Archives & Special Collections, J.D. Williams Library, University of Mississippi.

409. Carter, interview with Jack Carter.

410. Hodding Carter III, interview conducted by Blackside, Inc.

411. Carter, interview by Jack Carter

412. Carter, interview conducted by Blackside.

413. Carter, interview conducted by Blackside.

414. Carter, interview by Courtney Brennan.

415. Harkey, *Burning Crosses*, p. 225

416. Ira Harkey, *Burning Crosses* (Bloomington, IN.: Xlibris, 2005), p. 14.

417. Ira Harkey, "Confusing Times, Dangerous Times," *Pascagoula Chronicle*, 18 September 1982.

418. Harkey, *Burning Crosses*, p. 18.

419. Obituary: Ira Harkey Jr./Mississippi Editor Back Integration, Oct. 6, 2006. Available: http://www.post-gazette.com/news/obituaries/2006/10/11/Obituary-Ira-Harkey-Jr-Mississippi-editor-backed-integration/stories/200610110137.

420. Gene Roberts and Hank Klibanoff, *The Race Beat: The Press, the Civil Rights Struggle, and the Awakening of a Nation.* (New York: Knopf, 2006),

421. "On Mississippi," *Columbia Journalism Review*, Winter 1963, pp. 2-3.

422. Nick Marinello and Michael DeMocker, Ira Harkey's War of Words, *Tulanian*, July 13, 2004.

423. Harkey, *Burning Crosses*, p. 225.

424. Mark Newman, "Hazel Brannon Smith and Holmes County, Mississippi, 1936-1964: The Making of a Pulitzer Prize Winner," *Journal of Mississippi History* 54 (February 1992): 59-87.

425. Newman, "Hazel Brannon Smith and Holmes County, Mississippi."

426. Hank Klibanoff, Dedication of the Paul L. Guihard Bench, University of Mississippi, transcript, April 17, 2009.

427. "The Press: The Last Word," *Time*, November 21, 1955; David Davies, "Mississippi Journalists, the Civil Rights Movement, and the Closed Society, 1960-1964" (paper presented at the 1994 convention of the American Journalism Historians Association, Roanoke, Va.). Available: http://ocean.otr.usm.edu/~w304644/missjourn.html.

428. Jan Whitt, *Burning Crosses and Activist Journalism: Hazel Brannon Smith and the Mississippi Civil Rights Movement* (New York: University Press of America, 2010).

429. "The Press: The Last Word," *Time*, November 21, 1955.

430 Wendy M. Reed, "Hazel Brannon Smith: A Portrait Of The Journalist As A Young Woman" (Ph.D. diss., University of Alabama, 2010).

431 Bernard L. Stein, "This Female Crusading Scalawag," *Media Studies Journal* 14, no. 2 (Spring/Summer 2000): 51-59.

432. "Governor Barnett Should Quit Now," *Lexington (Miss.) Advertiser*, 27 September 1962.

433. World and Nation's Press Comment on Ole Miss, *Lexington (Miss.) Advertiser*, 18 October 1962.

434. Hazel Brannon Smith, "Through Hazel Eyes," *Lexington (Miss.) Advertiser*, 18 October 1962.

435. "Prizes: Just Doing the Job," *Time*, May 15, 1964.

436. Reed, "Hazel Brannon Smith."

437. Juan Williams, "The Truth Shall Make You Free: The Mississippi Free Press, 1961-63," *Journalism History* 32, no. 2 (Summer 2006): 106-113.

438. Stein, "This Female Crusading Scalawag."

439. Michael L. Cooper, "Bill Minor's Forty-Five Years of Progressive Journalism," *Southern Changes* 14, no. 3 (1992): 12-17.

440. Cooper, "Bill Minor's Forty-Five Years of Progressive Journalism."

441. "The Sound and the Fury," *Newsweek*, October 15, 1962.

442. Cooper, "Bill Minor's Forty-Five Years of Progressive Journalism."

443. Jerry Mitchell, "Ten days ago, veteran journalist Bill Minor quietly celebrated his 81st birthday," *The (Jackson, Miss.) Clarion-Ledger*, May 27, 2003.

444. Lucy Komisar, email message to author, June 5, 2013.

445. Lucy Komisar, "A personal history of civil rights and feminism," panel, transcript, *Women, Queens College and the Civil Rights Movement*, 16 March 2009, Queens College, University of Southern Mississippi, Lucy Komisar Civil Rights Collection, McCain Library and Archives, University of Southern Mississippi.

446. Komisar, interview by Julie Altman, Tully-Crenshaw Feminist Oral History Project, Schlesinger Library, Radcliffe College, 16 October 1991, provided by Lucy Komisar, 30 November 30, 2012.

447. Seth Cagin and Philip Dray, *We Are Not Afraid*, (New York: Nation Books, 2006).

448. Komisar, *Women, Queens College and the Civil Rights Movement*.

449. "A Newspaper is Born," *Mississippi Free Press*, December 16, 1961, 1, Lucy Komisar Civil Rights Collection, McCain Library and Archives, University of Southern Mississippi.

450. Komisar, interview by Julie Altman.

451. Komisar.

452. Charles Butts, interview with author, February 1, 2013.

453. Komisar, "Women, Queens College and the Civil Rights Movement."

454. Lucy Komisar, interview with author, January 23, 2013.

455. Charles Butts, interview with author, February 1, 2013.

456. Lucy Komisar, email message to author, June 5, 2013.

457. Komisar, interview by Julie Altman.

458. Lucy Komisar, interview with author, January 23, 2013.

459. Komisar, interview.

460. "Meredith in College; Doesn't Take Never," *Mississippi Free Press*, October 6, 1962.

461. Butts, interview with author.

462. Sophie McNeil, "It Won't Be Long," *Jackson (Miss.) Free Press*, 18 May 2011.

463. HiCo Publishing Company, Charter of Incorporation, Mississippi Department of Archives and History, Mississippi Sovereignty Commission, SCR ID 3-76-0-10-2-1-1.

464. Butts, interview.

465. Charles Butts, interview by Louis Massiah, transcript, Eyes on the Prize II, Henry Hampton Collection, Film and Media Archive, Washington University, St. Louis, Mo., October 29, 1988, Accessed December 18, 2012, http://digital.wustl.edu/e/eii/eiiweb/but5427.0198.026marc_record_interviewee_process.html.

466. Butts, interview.

467. Butts.

468. Butts.

RESEARCH ESSAY

Almost 10 years ago I made my first foray into the world of archives and research libraries, starting with the National Archives located in southeast Georgia. My quest at that time was focused on the records of the U.S. Marshals Service. When I arrived staffers told me that since the files had arrived decades earlier no one had searched them for material related to the Meredith case. A few years later, when I returned, the pale blue paper I had inserted in files to note where I wanted to make copies remained; apparently in the intervening years no one had touched the files.

A Freedom of Information request filed with the U.S. Department of Justice resulted in a 2,000-page DOJ file on James Meredith. Much is redacted but when matched with the U.S. Marshal files much was learned.

The depth and breadth of archival materials, starting with the Department of Archives and Special Collections at the University of Mississippi, the McCain Library and Archives at Southern Mississippi University, Special Collections at the Mississippi State Library and the Mississippi Department of Archives and History, was significant.

At Baylor University's Institute for Oral History I located lost oral histories gathered during the 1987 conference on civil rights at The University of Mississippi. The lost transcripts from the conference were also at Baylor. These are being returned to the Ole Miss library. Washington University in St. Louis awarded me a research grant so I could spend a week exploring the Eyes on the Prize collection housed in its Film & Media Archives. All three archives provided a wealth of authentic primary material.

Memos, institutional files and research papers were found in the Department of Manuscripts, Archives and Rare Books at the New York City Public Library and at the Rare Book and Manuscript Library at Columbia University. Special Collections at the University of Memphis and at the Memphis & Shelby County Public Library provided files of news clippings. Oral histories, speeches, memos and news clippings which provided content, nuance and significance were found at numerous libraries, including the S.I. Newhouse School of Public Communications at Syracuse University; the Manuscript, Archives and Rare Book Library at Emory University; Special Collections and University Archives at SUNY-Stonybrook; Archives & Collections at the University of Virginia; the Archives department at Washington State University; and the archives at York Library, Toronto, Canada.

The John F. Kennedy Presidential Library in Boston provided detailed information related to the federal government's plans and actions in 1962, especially its collection of presidential audio tapes and transcripts of the March 1998 Forum on Press Coverage of the American Civil Rights Movement.

Various University of Mississippi institutional programs generated oral histories, memories, context and answers. The September 2012 program, 50 Years of Integration: Opening the Closed Society, brought many participants back to campus for programs, seminars and interviews. Their voices added authenticity to the manuscript as well as context.

Additional primary material was gathered from three other programs held at the University of Mississippi: The Paul Guihard Memorial Bench Dedication in April 2009, Dan Rather's address at Without Fear and With Courage: Honoring the Reporters who covered the Ole Miss Integration Crisis in April 2010 and John Seigenthaler's talk given at the Inside the Lyceum September 30, 1962 program held in September 2010.

Syracuse University's S.I. Newhouse School of Public Communications Civil Rights and The Press Symposium program in April 2004 provided primary material as did the Newseum's program Inside Media: James Meredith and the Integration of Ole Miss and the March Against Fear in June 2016.

The "sweetest" moment may have occurred at the Archives and Special Collections department at Harvard University's Houghton Library. There, the day after graduation, all researchers in the archives were invited out to the lobby for tea, cookies and conversation.

Supplementing the transcripts and oral histories were interviews with participants. Gathering the interviews was challenging. Many had left the journalism profession and could not be located, a few others were too ill to be interviewed and a significant number had passed during the last 55 years. Oral histories filled in the gaps. Over the last decade the following journalists and contributors were interviewed: Sidna Brower, Moses Newson, Tom Brown, Effie Burt, Charles Butts, Dorothy Gilliam, Neal Gregory, Alain Guihard, Lucy Komisar, the Rev. Michel Leutellier, Bill Minor, Charles Moore, Claude Sitton, Fred Powledge, Richard Valeriani, and Kay Veasey.

Due diligence was practiced in identifying copyright holders for the photographs. Ed Meek's photographs were provided courtesy of the Meek School of Journalism & New Media at The University of Mississippi. Alain Guihard provided the photographs of his brother Paul Guihard. The profiled reporters or their family members provided some photographs. Other photographs were found in various archives and libraries, including Archives and Special Collections at The University of Mississippi, the Flip Schulke Archive at the University of Texas-Austin and the National Press Photographers Association.

SELECTED BIBLIOGRAPHY

Ashmore, Harry Ashmore. "Covering History as It Broke: John N. Popham." *Southern Changes*, vol. 6, no. 1 (1984).

Blotner, Joseph, ed. Selected letters of William Faulkner. New York: Random House, 1977.

Cagin, Seth Cagin and Dray, Philip. *We Are Not Afraid*. New York: Nation Books, 2006.

Commission on the Freedom of the Press (Hutchins Commission). *A Free and Responsible Press*, Chicago: The University of Chicago Press, 1947.

de Sola, Ithiel and Shulman, Irwin, "Newsmen's fantasies, audiences, and newswriting," *Public Opinion Quarterly* 23 (summer 1959) 145:58.

Dorman, Michael. *We Shall Overcome*. New York: Delacote Press, 1964.

Doyle, William. *An American Insurrection: The Battle of Oxford, Mississippi, 1962*. New York: Doubleday, 2001.

Faulkner, William. *The Sound and the Fury*. New York: Jonathan Cape & Harrison Smith, 1929.

Faulkner, William. *Intruder in the Dust*. New York: Random House, 1948.

Feinstein, Anthony. "The psychological hazards of war," *Neiman Reports* 58, no. 2 (Summer 2004).

Fleming, Karl. *Son of the Rough South*. New York: Public Affairs, 2005.

Hamblin, Robert W. *Myself and the World: A biography of William Faulkner*, Jackson: University Press of Mississippi, 2016.

Harkey, Ira. *Burning Crosses*. Bloomington, IN.: Xlibris, 2005.

Haygood, Wil. "Story Of Their Lives; For Reporters on the Civil Rights Beat, The Trick Was to Cover The News, Not Be It." *The Washington Post*, 26 November 2006.

Herbers, John. "The Reporter in the Deep South, *Nieman Reports* 56, no. 2 (April 1962): 3

Hooker, Robert Wright. *Race and the News Media in Mississippi*, 1962-1964 (master's thesis, Vanderbilt University, 1971).

Johnston, Araminta Stone. *And One was a Priest: The Life and Times of Duncan M. Gray Jr.* Jackson: University Press of Mississippi, 2001.

Jones, John Griffin. *Mississippi Writers Talking: Interviews with Eudora Welty, Shelby Foote, Elizabeth Spencer, Barry Hannah, Beth Henley*. Jackson, University Press of Mississippi, 1982.

Lally, Kathy. "A journey from racism to reason: The Clarion-Ledger of Jackson, Miss." *The Baltimore Sun Journal*, 5 January 1997.

Leonard, George B., Harris, T. George and Wren, Christopher S. "How a Secret Deal Prevented a Massacre at Ole Miss," *Look*, December 31, 1962.

Massie, Robert. "What Next in Mississippi." *Saturday Evening Post*, November 10, 1962.

McKown, Ted. "Faulkner Talks to Reporters about Integration, Virginians, Charlotte Daily Progress," In *Conversations with William Faulkner*, ed. M. Thomas Inge. Jackson: University Press of Mississippi, 1999.

Newman, Mark. "Hazel Brannon Smith and Holmes County, Mississippi, 1936-1964: The Making of a Pulitzer Winner. *Journal of Mississippi History* 54 (February 1992): 59-87.

"On Mississippi." *Columbia Journalism Review*, Winter 1963, pp. 2-3.

Patronik, Michael. "Newspaper Coverage of the Desegregation of Southern Universities." master's thesis, University of Mississippi, 2011.

"Prize Winner." *Journal of Mississippi History* 54 (February 1992): 59-87.

Rather, Dan. *The Camera Never Blinks*. New York: William Morrow, 1977.

Reed, Wendy M. Reed. "Hazel Brannon Smith: A Portrait Of The Journalist As A Young Woman." Ph.D. diss., University of Alabama, 2010.

Roberts, Gene and Klibanoff, Hank. *The Race Beat: The Press, the Civil Rights Struggle, and the Awakening of a Nation*. New York: Knopf, 2006.

Schulke, Flip. *Witness to Our Times*. Chicago: Cricket Books, 2003.

Schulman, Sammy. *Where's Sammy?* New York: Random House, 1943.

Silver, James. *Mississippi: The Closed Society*. New York: Harcourt, Brace & World, 1964.

Slappey, Sterling and Trikosko Marion S. "I Saw It Happen in Oxford." *U.S. News & World Report*, October 15, 1962.

Stein, Bernard L. "This Female Crusading Scalawag." *Media Studies Journal* 14, no. 2 (Spring/Summer 2000): 51-59.

Sugrue, Thomas J. *Sweet Land of Liberty: The Forgotten Struggle for Civil Rights in the North*. New York: Random House, 2008.

Thomas, Evan. *Robert Kennedy: His Life*. New York: Simon & Shuster, 2000.

"Though the heavens fall." *Time*, October 12, 1962, 20.

Whitt, Jan. *Burning Crosses and Activist Journalism: Hazel Brannon Smith and the Mississippi Civil Rights Movement*. New York: University Press of America, 2010.

United States. Kerner Commission, Report of the National Advisory Commission on Civil Disorders (Washington: U.S. Government Printing Office, 1968).

Weill, Susan Weill. *In a Madhouse's Din: Civil Rights Coverage by Mississippi's Daily Press, 1948-1968*. Westport, Conn.: Praeger, 2002.

Wickham, Kathleen Woodruff. *The Role of the Clarion-Ledger in the adoption of the 1982 Education Reform Act*. Lewiston, N.Y.: The Edwin Mellen Press, 2007.

Williams, Juan Williams. "The Truth Shall Make You Free: The Mississippi Free Press, 1961 63." *Journalism History 32*, no. 2 (Summer 2006): 106-113.

ACKNOWLEDGEMENTS

Literary history surrounded me as I revised and polished this book at the home of William Faulkner's parents in Oxford, Mississippi, working at the same table where Faulkner edited the galley proofs of his novel *Absalom, Absalom.*

For this opportunity I have to thank my publisher, Larry Wells. Larry agreed to publish my manuscript six months before we met. He saw my vision and, with his deft editing skills, helped me infuse the book with the techniques of literary journalism, more befitting the topic than my previous journalistic approach.

We Believed We Were Immortal developed from my interest in the 1962 murder of Paul Guihard. While researching his story I stumbled across the Western Union Telegram Collection housed in Archives and Special Collections at The University of Mississippi. There, in raw stories, were the emotions and experiences of covering the integration riot that is the core of the manuscript. I wanted the reporters' words to drive the story, not my interpretation of their polished work. It has been a six-year journey to reach that goal.

I wish to extend my appreciation to Dr. Will Norton, dean of the Meek School of Journalism & New Media at The University of Mississippi, for granting me a sabbatical in Fall 2011, and to Associate Dean Charlie Mitchell for finding research and travel funds. A research grant in summer 2011 enabled me to focus on research instead of summer school. Travel money enabled me to visit archives across the South and East Coast and to interview Alain Guihard in St. Malo, France, where the brothers spent their youth during World War II.

I wish to express my deepest gratitude to the following: the librarians who answered my queries, found files and suggested other resources; Alain Guihard, whom I located through a Google search and kindly shared photographs and memories; Marie Gerard of Strasbourg, France, for facilitating the French connection; and Sidna Brower, who was always ready for yet another interview. I met Dan Rather when he volunteered his time to speak at the School program noting the designation of the Ole Miss campus as a National Historic Site in Journalism. Hank Klibanoff, co-author of *The Race Beat*, also volunteered his time, speaking at the dedication of the Guihard memorial bench on campus. Jerry Mitchell of *The Clarion-Ledger*, whose work has brought many former Klan members to justice, encouraged me, as did the late John Siegenthaler, who served under Attorney General Robert Kennedy, and was beaten by racist thugs in Birmingham. William Doyle, author of *An American Insurrection*, and Henry Gallagher, author of *James Meredith and the Ole Miss Riot: A Soldier's Story*, shared many conversations with me about September 30, 1962, providing additional clarity about the events.

Students and staff at the School of Journalism provided assistance and editorial support, including Shannon Dixon, Paula Hurdle, Ellen Everett, Julie Baker, Faith Hogarty, Mallory Simerville Lehenbauer, Silpa Swarnapuri, Ariel Booker, Ellen Kellum, Maren O'Haver, Hunter Thompson, Rachel Moffett and Andrew Scott. I wish to express my appreciation for their assistance. Peter Mattiace's editing suggestions were invaluable.

Finally, I wish to thank my friends who have listened to me talk about this project for years with a lot of patience; my sons, Matthew and Timothy, and grandson Liam for their love; and my parents, Ann and Ralph Woodruff, who valued reading and learning above everything else.

Oxford, Mississippi
September 30, 2017

INDEX

ABOUT THE AUTHOR

Dr. Kathleen Woodruff Wickham is professor of journalism at The University of Mississippi where she teaches Advanced Reporting, Media Ethics, Magazine Writing and a course on press coverage of civil rights. She has also lectured at the Sorbonne and Rennes universities in France. She previously taught at The University of Memphis and worked as a reporter at the *Newark (N.J.) Star-Ledger and Atlantic City (N.J.) Press.* She was instrumental in having the Society of Professional Journalists designate The University of Mississippi a national historic site in journalism in honor of the reporters who covered the 1962 integration crisis and establish a memorial marker in honor of the Paul Guihard, the French reporter murdered on campus during the 1962 riot. She has published three books, numerous academic articles and since 2010 has judged the National Headliner Journalism Awards. In 2008 SPJ presented Wickham the David L. Eshelman National Outstanding Campus Adviser Award.

This book is set in a melange of Century (Extended, Schoolbook, and Gothic) in an effort to balance historical verisimilitude with modern aesthetics.

Printed on 120 gsm Neo Star white text paper by Four Color Print Group.